The Text of

MONUMENTAL
CLASSIC ARCHITECTURE
IN
GREAT BRITAIN
AND IRELAND

THE CLASSICAL AMERICA SERIES IN
ART AND ARCHITECTURE

Henry Hope Reed and H. Stafford Bryant, Jr.,
General Editors

The American Vignola, by William R. Ware

The Architecture of Humanism, by Geoffrey Scott

The Classic Point of View, by Kenyon Cox

The Decoration of Houses, by Edith Wharton
and Ogden Codman, Jr.

*Fragments from Greek and Roman Architecture: The Classical America
edition of Hector d'Espouy's Plates*

The Golden City, by Henry Hope Reed

The Library of Congress: Its Architecture and Decoration
by Herbert Small

Monumental Classic Architecture in Great Britain and Ireland,
by Albert E. Richardson

THE CLASSICAL AMERICA PERIODICAL

Classical America IV, edited by William A. Coles
(published as a book in 1978)

Classical America is the society which encourages the classical
tradition in the arts of the United States. Inquiries about the society
should be sent to Classical America, in care of W. W. Norton & Company, Inc.
500 Fifth Avenue, New York, N.Y. 10110.

The general editors would like especially to thank
Dr. David Watkin and John Barrington Bayley
for their assistance towards preparation of this edition.

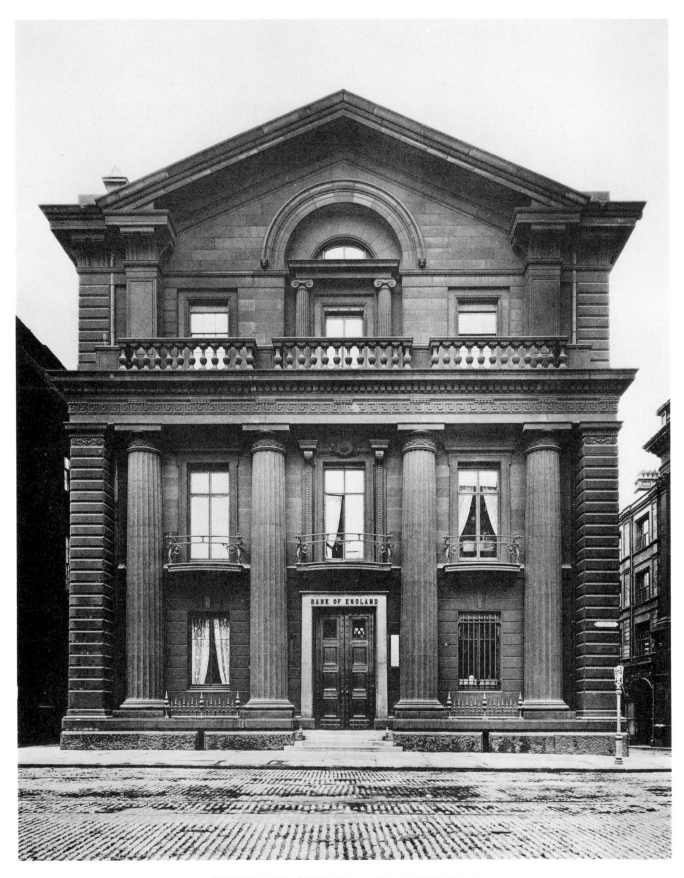

THE BANK OF ENGLAND. LIVERPOOL.

PROFESSOR C. R. COCKERELL R.A. ARCHITECT.

MONUMENTAL CLASSIC ARCHITECTURE IN GREAT BRITAIN AND IRELAND

ALBERT E. RICHARDSON

A NEW EDITION

Introductory Notes by

H. STAFFORD BRYANT, JR.

W. W. NORTON & COMPANY
NEW YORK · LONDON

ISBN 0-393-01451-7 cloth
ISBN 0-393-00053-2 pbk.
W. W. Norton & Company, Inc. 500 Fifth Avenue, New York, N.Y. 10110
W. W. Norton & Company Ltd. 37 Great Russell Street, London WC1B 3NU

1 2 3 4 5 6 7 8 9 0

CONTENTS

Comments by the Sponsor

"... the monumental in architecture as in nature is universal, it is eternal, and it is true." This bold statement is at the heart of Sir Albert E. Richardson's ennobling and exhilarating book *Monumental Classic Architecture in Great Britain and Ireland*. This period represented the brilliant culmination and conspicuous formation of a high standard of taste. It eloquently demonstrated that the classical had survived the test of time and had received the approbation of the ages.

Mr. Richardson's book, illustrated with plates, drawings and photographs, eloquently links man's classical architectural efforts to the grandeur of nature. It is nature, he states, which compelled man "to feast his eyes on splendid distances, inaccessible heights and impressive depths—and from the terrific contrasts in her honest countenance, provided man with his early inspirations." The amateur and the professional will sense the prevailing spirit of encouragement and elevation in this book and will be invigorated and ennobled by it.

The Arthur Ross Foundation, in cooperation with Classical America, is pleased to have the opportunity to make this edition possible as part of the Series in Art and Architecture. It is one of a series on Classical Architecture sponsored by the Arthur Ross Foundation and Classical America. Both the Foundation and Classical America hope these publications will contribute to an increased awareness of our classical roots and to their renewed influence in the architectural schools of America.

New York City
August 1, 1981

ARTHUR ROSS

INTRODUCTORY NOTES

RICHARDSON'S *MONUMENTAL CLASSIC ARCHITECTURE* AS A TRACT FOR THE TIMES, by H. Stafford Bryant, Jr., director, classical america

THE buildings, gardens and planning of Great Britain have been so thoroughly photographed, studied, written about, mapped, and analyzed that pound for pound and square yard for square yard it must be the best-known architecture in the world. England leads the world in guides to and histories of its houses, gardens, parish churches, and public buildings, and has for decades. Try, for instance, to find a guide to French or Spanish castles that is handy and compact, and you will appreciate the several excellent publications of the English National Trust. And there is hardly anything comparable in the rest of the world to the literature of the English parish church, cathedral, or abbey, or to the literature of the English dwelling, large or small. Certainly the systematic study of American building lags far behind that of England.

But there is, even at this late date, a more or less neglected phase in the study of British building—neglected except for this unusual and, as it turns out, unique volume. Sir Albert Edward Richardson's *Monumental Classic Architecture in Great Britain and Ireland During the XVIIIth and XIXth Centuries** is, in its most literal sense, a survey of monumental public building in those places from about 1730 over the succeeding 150 years. More than that, Richardson made his book a carefully argued *tract* in favor of his particular and special notions as to what constitutes excellence in classical architecture. Richardson's ideas of quality in building are extremely clear, and he starts his book by setting his time limits firmly. His first eligible building—Richard Cassell's Parliament House in Dublin—dates from 1730–39, which means that Richardson has excluded such early giants of English classicism as Inigo Jones, Vanbrugh, and Christopher Wren. His monumental classic has run its course by 1875, and none of the luminaries of Edwardian architecture receives his imprimatur or even his mention.

Indeed Richardson's omissions and critical slights are extremely significant and may be devastating to some. It is worth pondering about the architects to whom he gives faint praise or censure and those he feels unworthy of inclusion at all. Of Wren, Richardson first gives lavish praise but then tempers it with lukewarm caveats: "Wren could not emancipate himself from the loose ornamental tendencies of [his] period." And again: Wren is "within certain bounds tolerably conversant with good Roman detail." (All of which squares with this writer's feeling that while Wren's St. Paul's has enormous charm and is overall a stunning urban amenity, the detailing is often irrational, naïve, or given to quirks of design. Throughout the building, some of the elements that a first-rate French or Italian architect of Wren's period would have included are missing.)

And read Richardson's sharp words on the architects of the Adam family: He first speaks of Robert Adam as "the brilliant Scotsman," but then says of the Adams that "they seldom adapted the orders and in many instances these features when employed in their designs are deficient in impressiveness . . . in brief, they belonged to the ornamental rather than the monumental school, sacrificing grandeur of conception to elegant mannerism." Strong stuff, and revealing of what is apparent on every page of *Monumental Classic Architecture:* that Richardson analyzes every building or detail, regardless of the fame or reputation of the architect involved, with his own stern critical apparatus.

Perhaps even more interesting are the silences at the end of Richardson's book. He feels that the history of English architecture from the year 1870 on, or at least until the decade 1905–15, consists of "a series of attempts to revive the various styles, each more or less provincial in their handling. For a time the academic aspect of Classic architecture has been partially interrupted, its truths have suffered censure as being ephemeral and fallacious." Evidently Richardson felt that such Edwardian luminaries as

*The title has been shortened for this edition.

MONUMENTAL ARCHITECTURE

Aston Webb (the East front of Buckingham Palace) and John Brydon (governmental buildings, Parliament Square, Westminster) failed to measure up, or at least he felt so when he wrote this book. Even more interesting is his omission of such a celebrity as Edwin Landseer Lutyens, who has become such an extraordinary cult figure in English art history. It may have been that Richardson felt that Lutyens' detailing, whenever it could be called classical at all, was bizarre and quirky. Certainly Richardson passes over such famous Victorians as Norman Shaw and Philip Webb, and with good reason, since they used classical as more or less cement or noggin in their various architectural pastiches.

Members of Classical America will be delighted to read Richardson's fulsome praise of McKim, Mead, and White. He writes: ". . . we have only to review the great strides made in recent years in America to understand the advantages of an academic school. It is this modern rendering of the antique style which lends such charm and interest to the monumental works of McKim, Mead and White; their work is great because it has assimilated something of the greatness which hovers over these ancient buildings constituting the standard of taste for the world. America [Richardson is writing in the first part of this century] is slowly but surely creating unto herself a distinct style; and one, moreover, which is excellent in architectural value because it embraces the theory of the Classic spirit without being a return to mere mechanical pedantry." Elsewhere he says, "The modern Classic movement in America is already a powerful agency and spur to the arts of Europe."

Richardson offers a very good brief guide to the four stylistic periods of his *Monumental Classic Architecture* in his Conclusion (VI). His periods or phases are: the Roman Palladian phase, 1730–1780; the Graeco-Roman phase, 1780–1820; the Greek phase, 1820–1840; and the Neo-Grec and Italian phase, 1840 on. This somewhat shifting and sliding terminology may at first seem confusing, but it does indicate how much all of the architects discussed in the book drew on Greek, Roman, and Renaissance sources. Study of the book makes the categories seem sensible and even inevitable.

The major figures of Richardson's first period—his Roman-Palladian phase—are Sir William Chambers and James Gandon. Richardson praised Chambers and Gandon for their "fuller acceptance of the antique spirit. Their buildings are original compositions, owing nothing more than the permeating spirit to the style which inspired their design." Moving his attention to the later eighteenth century, Richardson saw publication of the researches of Stuart and Revett, *Antiquities of Athens*, as giving a "new impetus to the arts of Europe" and as preparing the way "for the rigid architectural discipline of the early years of the nineteenth century." The Neo-Grec phase, third in Richardson's succession of four, produced Nash and Smirke, saw the importation of the Elgin marbles, and "finally saw public opinion to be used on Greece." But Richardson saw the Greek period as lacking warmth, "which is among the attributes of fine art."

It is clear that Richardson saw his final period—the Neo-Grec and Italian—as the most fruitful time for English monumental classic architecture and as the day of the greatest masters of the whole movement, whom he cited as Harry Lonsdale Elmes and Professor Charles Robert Cockerell. Richardson argues that Elmes and Cockerell "more than ever achieved that elusive and subtle quality, rightness of character." "Rightness of character" is certainly a compelling phrase, comparable to the "suitability" of Edith Wharton and Ogden Codman in *The Decoration of Houses*.

The writer of this essay takes issue with some of Richardson's enthusiasm for the English Neo-Grec and Italian phase, as will be explained below, but it is most certainly this period—the age of Elmes and Cockerell, as well as of Sir Charles Barry—that offers many of the most interesting aspects of English classical for the follower of Classical America.[1] In the first place, English architects and builders achieve the grand scale of European classical with such buildings as St. George's Hall, Liverpool, and the Fitzwilliam Museum, Cambridge, a trend that continued into the Edwardian period with the great governmental buildings of the Whitehall district of London. The Neo-Grec phase is also characterized by the great abundance of classical sculpture (including, in many cases, free-standing statuary) in the heroic mode, offered as an integral feature of the buildings they accompany. The most prominent examples of sculpture used in English monumental classical include the whole of St. George's Hall, in which it is used in abundance both within and along the façades. In a similar category is the sculptural "program" in the tympanum of the Royal Exchange, London; the statuary on the roof line of the National Bank of England, Threadneedle Street, London; and the figures capping the columns of the Taylor and Randolph Buildings, Oxford (now the Ashmolean Museum). Fine sculpture was also part of some of the buildings of the first phase of Richardson's monumental classic, most conspicuously in Chambers' Somerset House. Another

INTRODUCTORY NOTES

prominent feature of English monumental is the use of the fully developed classical ceiling, with coffering and often gilding; St. George's Hall is the example par excellence.

On the other hand, there is nothing in Richardson's English monumental classical to compare with the grand scheme of mural painting so conspicuously a feature of the American Library of Congress in Washington.

Richardson is very concerned with defining just what constitutes monumental or academic architecture, and his notions are instructive. It is the duty of the artist, he writes, "to inquire into the cult of the monumental to determine not only the universal laws which govern its evolution but to establish an academic rule which can be applied to any particular manifestation of it. To review the many forms of architecture from a critical standpoint, to subject them to drastic comparison with those which have survived the test of time and received the approbation of the ages, is the surest method of judgment."

Richardson believes that the monumental and academic building he would put forward as worthwhile examples for contemporary architects to follow has a specific origin and has a particular function in urbanism. For Richardson, the true monumental in England began after the age of Wren, and its impetus came from the archaeological work and other scholarly activities in the circle of collectors, amateurs, and architects around Lord Burlington, most of whom sought to have architecture return to the monumental style of Rome. Later, at the beginning of the nineteenth century, or in Richardson's Graeco-Roman phase, monumental resulted from a movement to study architecture on a wider scale, not only the Roman of ancient Italy but also the Greek and Hellenistic building of the Greek Archipelago and Asia Minor—the writings of Stuart and Revett being, of course, part of the move to study Greek architecture.

Richardson's prescription for the application of the monumental style to urban centers is a key passage from his texts and deserves quotation in full: "An academic style is necessary to the architecture of the great civic centers: without its benign and uplifting influence the correct tone of the capital can never be attained. All building partakes somewhat of the character which prevails at such culminating points of interest. Where else is it to obtain its impression? What else exists to be mirrored?"

Richardson was not above a certain amount of hyperbole, as this quotation illustrates nicely: "The ultimate success of a great architectural development depends, not on a series of individual and inflated movements, but in combined and sustained effort. There must be a common atmosphere in which all can participate. The resulting unity will be productive of the highest intellectual attainments, compared with which the fairest flowers of the Italian Renaissance will appear trivial." An extravagant claim, of course, but a clear statement of the true aim of Classical America and others who dream of seeing the classical spirit again prevail in the arts.

It seems almost obvious to say that Richardson's *Monumental Classic* is of great potential value to a modern architect or designer who would work in the classical. Not only does Richardson have sure philosophical ideas as to what makes for good classical building, but the book is a treasury of illustrations of fine examples, given Richardson's particular biases, over the 150 years of British architecture he is concerned with. The book deals with several types of buildings that a lucky classical architect might be asked to design. There are town halls, law court buildings, museums, governmental offices, libraries, assembly halls, all photographed beautifully by one E. Docktree in the grand Edwardian manner we associate with *Country Life* of the period. And there are, besides, many measured drawings, of details, plans and elevations.

The selections among classical building in Richardson's book can and should be viewed critically, and this writer means to attempt it. If, as Richardson's text indicates, English classical building had matured sufficiently to be worth the term monumental only by 1730, then this occurred a full century and a half after the Italian classical of Michelangelo and Palladio, and some two generations after the work of Perrault, Hardouin-Mansart, and Le Vau in France. The French, according to Richardson, "were the first to foresee the advantages that would accrue to the art of architecture by the formation of an academy. They possess to a very considerable degree an instinct for what is right and wrong in archi-

---

1. At one point Richardson puts his Neo-Grec and Italian phase into an international context. He cites Hittorff's Church of St. Vincent de Paul in Paris and the same architect's Gare du Nord, the library of Ste. Geneviève by Labrouste (which Richardson calls "exquisite"), and the library of the Ecole des Beaux-Arts by Duban. But his favorite abroad seems to have been the German Carl Fredrick Schinkel, whom he saw as an influence on Cockerell and Elmes. *Monumental Classic Architecture* does not mention American builders from the first three-quarters of the American nineteenth century, but the work of Benjamin Henry Latrobe would seem to fit into this pantheon.

Text Ill. I.
Somerset House, London.   Palladian Bridge motif by Sir William Chambers.

Text Ill. II.
Detail of elevation of Taylor and Randolph Building, Oxford
(now the Ashmolean Museum) by Professor C. R. Cockerell.

MONUMENTAL ARCHITECTURE

tectural matters; as a result there is to be seen in French architecture a remarkable consistency, a leveling up in favor of a general idea rather than an encouragement of haphazard individuality."

In this writer's opinion, the best achievements during the 150 years that *Monumental Classic Architecture* covers occurred during its beginning, or in what Richardson calls the Roman-Palladian phase. The book devotes eighteen illustrations to Sir William Chambers, who emerges from these pages as an absolute master of classical building, both in his detailing and in the general planning of his best buildings. What can be more sublime than the Casino Marino in Dublin, or the connecting bridges of his Somerset House in London? And the book offers other splendid exercises by lesser lights of the mid- and late Georgian period, such as Robert Taylor, James Gandon, and George Dance. In this period, note more of Richardson's silences: nothing pictured by such stalwarts as Kent, Gibbs,[2] Colin Campbell, Hawksmoor, or Thomas Archer, all of whom, to be sure, spent much of their energies doing houses and churches—which do not, of course, fall into Richardson's purview.

His succeeding period, which seems the least interesting in the book, covers the building of the early to mid-nineteenth century. Richardson has great praise for Sir John Soane, whom he sees as the essential link between the paladins of the mid-eighteenth century and those of the late nineteenth. Soane, in Richardson's view, had a genius for architectural forms and for good planning generally, excepting his occasional essays into free form or picturesque detailing. Nash, Richardson believes, was the creator of theatrical architecture, but in some respects his buildings are "insincere and lack the essentials of the monumental manner."

Any careful reader of *Monumental Classic Architecture* will find that praise of the architects of the mid-eighteenth century runs directly counter to Richardson's conclusions. As we have said, in his view the culmination of English classical comes during the final, or Neo-Grec and Italian, phase and in the work of Cockerell and Elmes. Richardson saw the greatest achievement of English monumental as being the grand St. George's Hall in Liverpool, for which Elmes was the main architect; on Elmes' death, Cockerell not only completed the building but furnished much of the design for the magnificent interiors. And indeed St. George's does seem a sublime achievement, with its almost perfect facade of Corinthian columns, the vast coffered ceiling, and the Corinthian order of its main interior. As such, it is a worthy model or example for a working classical achitect of today.

As for Cockerell's other works, which Richardson chronicles in *Monumental Classic Architecture*, they give this writer serious pause. Cockerell is something of a specially beloved architectural figure in England, much in the same way Lutyens is. He is the subject of an admiring biography by David Watkin, the English architectural historian, and has been praised and honored by Sir John Summerson. But let us consider Cockerell's Taylor and Randolph Building at Oxford, now the Ashmolean Museum. The free-standing Ionic columns supporting entablatures have almost the character of gothic buttresses or even structural supports in some Bauhaus exercise, and the buildings are full of curious ornament. The Ionic capitals are oddly modeled, to say the very least, and the reliefs on the convex frieze member seem more Coptic or Arabic than classical. "Odd" or "curious" seems the word also for the relief plaques set into the attic of the side façades and for the lunette windows fitted harshly between the statues. Original certainly, but it is classical?

Richardson greatly admires Cockerell's London and Globe offices in Liverpool (Plate XLIII). Here Cockerell seems to have taken a loving look at the buildings of Giulio Romano, Raphael, and other Italians of the manneristic persuasion and then to have created a most disagreeable façade. Consider the ponderous use of swag ornament; the curious pedimental windows of the top story at the ends of each façade; the free-form use of rustication, or the sunken and cramped corbels. Again, original (for better or worse), but hardly classical.

Cockerell's Bank of England offices at both Manchester (Plate XLII) and Bristol (Plate XLII) seem much more felicitous, although they too stretch the meaning of the term "classical." Perhaps that thoroughly illogical but hard-to-avoid term "stripped classical" applies here. (Strictly speaking, classical can never be "stripped" since it must always use the full classical vocabulary of ornament.) In any case, Cockerell's banks closely suggest the later work of the American Paul Cret, in which Cret moved away from his early classical efforts to a style that was most certainly stripped and is generally regarded as being "art deco" (or the Rockefeller Center style).

---

2. In an omission that seems particularly baffling, Richardson fails to picture or cite Gibbs' Senate House at Cambridge (1722–30), though he does praise Gibbs' Radcliffe Library at Oxford (particularly the magnificent exterior).

INTRODUCTORY NOTES

As for his interiors, Cockerell seems to come off better. His entrance hall to the Fitzwilliam Museum at Cambridge (Plate XLVI) achieves some of the grandeur and poshness of the French Second Empire. It is a fine exercise in the style of the Paris Opera, with a variety of marbles and ormulu mouldings, rosettes and cartouches. And, again, there is Cockerell's work for St. George's Hall, which seems worthy of all of the superlative phrases Richardson uses in describing it: "Dignity," "Dorian Simplicity and grandeur," "voluptuous elegance."

Estimates as to the quality of the actual buildings aside, it is in his discussion of the Neo-Grec and Italian phase—the period that produced the major works of Cockerell, Elmes, and Sir Charles Barry—that Richardson makes his most telling intellectual points. His apology for the Neo-Grec movement is well worth reviewing, and it is of great interest and importance to those who would continue to build in the classical modes (and hence the cause of Classical America). First, Richardson believes that by 1840 the English monumental classic movement has reached an apotheosis. He writes that the great architect-designers of the period, having mastered the Greek and Roman classical, could now free their imaginations from what he calls the "cumbersome machinery of archaeology." He says further:

"In these and many other laudable efforts, undertaken during a mechanical and commercial epoch, there is descernible something of the Homeric age, something eloquent of the idyllic Italian renaissance, and moreover something essentially modern. The names of Professor Cockerell, Harvey Lonsdale, Elmes and Sir Charles Barry are pre-eminent among those who, while they demonstrate the suitability of the Hellenic motif, avoided the pedantic reproduction of its forms. They review the architectural problems of their day with the eyes of the Greeks, full of appreciation for the purest sensuous beauty, never over-stepping the limits of the academic and thoroughly understanding the impartation of pure architectural character."

Richardson's masters of monumental classic were not all famous architects with commissions in London or the university towns. With Richardson's classical, as with classical building in the United States, much of the best of it is out of town, so to speak. We can see from his pages many of the buildings that make Edinburgh superlatively exciting for the lover of classical building; it is a city with not just one fine acropolis but several. Here Richardson is careful to make Thomas Hamilton, the author of the High School in Edinburgh, a figure of the same order as Chambers, Cockerell, or Elmes, calling him a genius at getting the "maximum effect of light and shade." And photographs of Hamilton's High School (Plate XXXI) do make it seem like a plate from d'Espouy's *Fragments from Greek and Roman Architecture*, so crisp and precise is the Grecian detailing.

All this is virtually as true of Dublin, which figures several times in the pages of *Monumental Classic Architecture* and lacks only the site features and marvelous hills of Edinburgh, although it does offer fine riverside vistas for its buildings. The provincial examples continue in Chester, Preston, Leith, and York. Almost inevitably, some of the key buildings from the period are to be found in Liverpool and Manchester, St. George's Hall being, of course, the most prominent example.

It is certainly tempting, in leafing through *Monumental Classic Architecture*, to speculate as to which American buildings may have been influenced by the various English examples he gives. (Obviously, the pastime of trying to spot architectural sources is, in the absence of clear documentation, a most perilous one.) The buildings of *Monumental Classic Architecture* do seem clearly to have influenced the look of New York City, at any rate. It is hard to see the Taylor and Randolph Buildings of Oxford (now the Ashmolean Museum) without thinking of Kent and Journalism halls at Columbia University—which do not, however, enjoy the benefit of connecting wing, and use classical motifs a little more conservatively than Cockerell was wont to do. The Oxford and Cambridge Club easily suggests a kinship with the Century Association in New York City, although the American building seems a more vigorous and interesting exercise than its English cousin. The influence of Barry's Reform and Traveler's clubs on the finer New York row-house brownstone of the mid-nineteenth century seems clear, especially in the use of a prominent roof cornice and pedimented windows with pronounced architrave surrounds—a correspondence pointed out by Henry Hope Reed.

Richardson's illustrations show some of the special English idiom in classical building. Here is often pictured the bold use of the keystone motif, which, at least since Vanbrugh's day, has taken on the character of a national eccentricity in English building, and has been used in many ways. At one point, Richardson amusingly praises John Carr, the York architect, for being free of "such eccentricities as gi-

Text Ill. III.
Title pages to original edition of *Monumental Classic Architecture in Great Britain and Ireland.*

MONUMENTAL CLASSIC ARCHITECTURE IN GREAT BRITAIN AND IRELAND DURING THE EIGHTEENTH & NINETEENTH CENTURIES

BY

A. E. RICHARDSON

Fellow of the Royal Institute of British Architects

ILLUSTRATED IN A SERIES OF PHOTOGRAPHS SPECIALLY TAKEN BY E. DOCKREE, & MEASURED DRAWINGS OF THE MORE IMPORTANT NEO-CLASSIC BUILDINGS, WITH DESCRIPTIVE TEXT

LONDON
B.T. BATSFORD, LTD. 94, HIGH HOLBORN
NEW YORK: CHAS. SCRIBNER'S SONS

Text Ill. IV.
Circular end.   St. George's Hall, Liverpool, by Harvey Lonsdale Elmes.

MONUMENTAL ARCHITECTURE

gantic keystones, absurd rustications and other redundancies." Another eccentricity is the repeated use of the ornamental swag. And there is always, for any Continental observer, the curious marriage of Italian and French monumental forms with the English sash window, which began as a device best suited to a cottage or small mansion but sometimes is blown up to a ludicrous size, in those cases in which the sash is used on a large building or palace.

Among its many virtues, *Monumental Classic Architecture* exists for simple pleasure, too. What a marvelous collection of buildings and designs of the very best aesthetic qualities!

H.S.B.

MONUMENTAL ARCHITECTURE

ABOUT SIR ALBERT E. RICHARDSON

A RECENT account of his career makes Sir Albert Richardson seem a sort of British Stanford White. The English writer Nicholas Taylor (see below) tells of Richardson's love of fast cars, bicycling, and elegant bric-a-brac, and writes: "His experienced courting of the world of big business, his outrageous use of the verbal pun, his rotund oratory, his smoking of equally rotund cigars—these were the essence of the Edwardian 'card,' a dining club man par excellence."

In his professional career, Richardson was infinitely less than White in one sense and infinitely more in another. His career as an architect left a modest inventory of monuments, not all of them fully classical. His classical masterpiece is most certainly the New Theatre in Manchester, a grand exercise in the tradition of the European opera house. His later works, which use classical ornament sparingly, parallel many American buildings of the same period. His Leith House, Gresham Street, London, and his much-admired St. Margaret's House, Wells Street, London (dating from 1931) abbreviate the classical orders: pilasters without fluting or developed capitals, or simplified entablatures. An obvious American comparison is the sort of building Paul Cret was designing in the thirties.

It is perhaps as an architectural critic, writer, and historian that Richardson will be longest remembered, and some of his books are very important indeed. His *Monumental Classic Architecture in Great Britain and Ireland* (reprinted here without changes in the text or plates, but with a shortened title) is a statement of purpose in classical building perhaps exceeded only by Geoffrey Scott's *The Architecture of Humanism*, among twentieth-century writings up to the end of World War II. Certainly no American of that period—a time when the United States seems to have led Britain substantially in the quality and amount of classical building—has come forward with any writing as forthright or as valuable. Curiously, a very different subject from classical building in the grand manner—English vernacular and minor architecture—absorbed the bulk of Richardson's scholarly energies. Such books as *The Smaller English House of the Later Renaissance: The English Inn: Past and Present*; and *Regional Architecture in the West of England* (all written with co-authors) are essential in the study of English minor or domestic building, to say nothing of the study of the English sources of American colonial building. Among his scholarly contributions in this field is an extensive list of measured drawings.

Richardson admired building of the American renaissance period, and he is known to have corresponded with Fiske Kimball, the curator and architectural historian, and later with Henry Hope Reed, now president of Classical America.

Richardson lived a long life that stretched from the late Victorian period to our own day, 1880–1965. In addition to his knighthood, he received ample honors during his lifetime. He was the son of a printer in Islington, London, and was educated modestly, first apprenticed to a surveyor and architect and later studying engineering and mechanical construction at Birkbeck College, London. In his later years, he lived in a certain amount of style at Ampthill in Bedfordshire.

The most complete account of his career is Nicholas Taylor's from *Edwardian Architecture and Its Origins*, edited by Alastair Service (London: Architectural Press, 1975). Taylor is sympathetic to Richardson and attempts to show how his career meshed into the complicated and busy world of Edwardian architects, with their clients and competitions. Richardson was the subject of a memoir by his grandson, Simon Houfe of Ampthill, England, which was published in England in 1980 (*Sir Albert Richardson, the Professor*).

The Text of

MONUMENTAL
CLASSIC ARCHITECTURE
IN
GREAT BRITAIN
AND IRELAND

PREFACE

THE object of the following pages is not to recount once more the history of Renaissance architecture in England : that can be followed in the standard works on the subject. Their object is rather to direct attention to the monumental qualities and academic aspect of Neo-Classic architecture, from the period of its inception at the beginning of the seventeenth century until the brilliant culmination during the second half of the nineteenth century. First, therefore, it is necessary to appreciate that architectural theory which acted as a stimulating creed and motive force to the whole movement ; to understand the precursory events which governed its interest and propagation ; to grasp the attitude of society towards the development and the conspicuous formation of a high standard of taste. Once this is clearly focussed, the way in which the main events follow each other and the reasons for their sequence and interlocking become apparent.

Although the subject embraces the important buildings designed by Inigo Jones and Sir Christopher Wren, the illustrations of the works of these masters are not given in this treatise, mainly because they have been adequately described by other authors, and to cover the same ground once more would be superfluous. In like manner, only the important buildings of the first half of the eighteenth century, such as come within the strict meaning of the term monumental, are included.

The monumental quality in architecture, as in all other aspects of art, is relative, and its definition depends on the proportion it bears to Nature's primal laws. Therefore it becomes the essential duty of the true artist to inquire into the cult of the monumental ; to determine not only the universal laws which govern its evolution, but to establish an academic rule which can be applied to any particular manifestation of it. To view the many forms of architecture from a critical standpoint, to subject them to drastic comparison with those which have survived the test of time and received the approbation of the ages, is the surest method of judgment. All the great works of art and literature are not only the product of intellectual creative activity, but owe some part of their lasting qualities to the refining function of constructive criticism.

In defining the meaning of the terms "academic" and "provincial" as applied to architecture I have made excerpts from Matthew Arnold's essay on "The Literary Influence of Academies," which has a distinct bearing on the practice of the arts.

Another reason why emphasis is given to that development of Neo-Classic architecture which followed the period of Sir Christopher Wren is because it embodies the earliest date at which both architects and amateurs sought to interpret the true Classic spirit. Under the aegis of Lord Burlington they tried to return to the refinement and the purity of composition, inherent in the monumental style of Rome. The outcome of this desire to transplant to England some part of the warmth of character of antique culture resulted in a passion for research, first in Italy and later in Greece. The Society of Dilettanti furthered the independent action of noblemen and their agents by organising archæological study and extending the sphere of operations to the Greek Archipelago and Asia Minor. After a time the Royal Academy came into existence, with its distinctive branches of architecture, sculpture, and painting. The Roman Palladian phase, initiated in Burlington's time, was succeeded by a Græco-Roman development mainly encouraged by the example of the Athenian researches. Hence through the remaining years of the eighteenth century until the close of the first quarter of the nineteenth the search for the sublime and lasting qualities of architecture continued. The vastness of the subject precludes my dealing with the numerous side issues which took place at intervals, but which had no great bearing on the trend of the main movement. In the Neo-Grec and Italian culmination, which occurred simultaneously with the rise of the Romantic school, there is to be seen the genesis of the modern cosmopolitan movement, the breaking down of the barriers of insular prejudice in favour of a broader understanding of architecture.

PREFACE

So strongly planted are the giant roots of the Classic growth that they withstood the successive shocks and storms occasioned by the uncertain tendencies of the second half of the last century, and to-day the tree promises a renewed blossoming. The need for the steadying influence of an academic style is more than apparent. There can be no question of revivals or revivifications ; such terms are erroneous ; but in the continuance of the spirit of the Classic tradition lies the greatest promise for the art of the future. I have endeavoured to avoid all controversial questions in my account of the monumental manner ; and with this idea in mind have selected the illustrations, which are the finest of their several types. In dealing with the lives of the architects who form the various groups in the history of the movement I have had recourse to a concise biographical arrangement which not only permits the career of any one architect to be understood in relation to the complete development, but also allows the inclusion of a list of works actually carried into being.

During recent years it seems remarkable that, while the domestic aspect of English architecture has received every consideration for its nurture and expansion, the more important practice of the monumental should have lapsed into desuetude. An academic style is necessary to the architecture of great civic centres : without its benign and uplifting influence the correct tone of the capital can never be attained. All building partakes somewhat of the character which prevails at such culminating points of interest. Where else is it to obtain its impression ? What else exists to be mirrored ? But when the tone at the centre of the city is decadent there concurs a corresponding depression on the outskirts. It is not my intention to urge the literal transference of the monumental quality to problems of domestic architecture ; that would be in direct contravention of the academic laws. Such methods were in vogue in the days of the Georges, and soon wrought their own destruction. Yet, notwithstanding, the grand style of domestic architecture has at all periods been influenced by the ennobling character of the monumental and the academic, and owes some part of its dignity to the style which pertains at the centre of taste.

The ultimate success of a great architectural development depends, not on a series of individual and isolated movements, but in combined and sustained effort. There must be a common atmosphere which all can breathe, a prevailing spirit of encouragement and elevation in which all can participate. The resulting unity of effort will be productive of the highest intellectual attainments, compared with which the fairest flowers of the Italian Renaissance will appear trivial.

A. E. RICHARDSON

41 RUSSELL SQUARE,
LONDON, W.C.
January 1914

NOTE OF ACKNOWLEDGMENT

I TAKE this opportunity of expressing my gratitude and obligation to all those who have afforded me their aid and advice in the production of this volume. The first place indubitably belongs to my friend and publisher, Mr. Herbert Batsford, whose enthusiasm for the fine arts and wide knowledge of English architecture assisted me to overcome many difficulties. His painstaking care and zealous help throughout the lengthy period of the book's preparation have been invaluable to me, and will be appreciated by all interested in the subject of this volume. Secondly, to Mr. E. Dockree, who visited with me the many buildings illustrated, and devoted many weeks of labour to secure the finest photographic results. To Mr. R. Phené Spiers I am indebted for advice and criticism, which I value the more because he, of all living Englishmen, has the most intimate knowledge of the architects of the second half of the last century. Mr. Walter Spiers has kindly afforded me facilities on many occasions to inspect drawings and volumes in the Soane Collection. I am indebted to Mr. Arthur Stratton for advice on both text and illustrations, to my partner, Mr. Charles Lovett Gill, for helpful criticism, and to Mr. A. E. Doyle, of Messrs. Batsford, for various suggestions during the production of the book.

For the loan of measured drawings and other data I thank my friends Leslie Wilkinson, Assistant Professor, of University College, Messrs. W. D. Quirke, Harold Hillier, Cecil Wright, Norbert Shaw, Charles Butt, G. G. Wornum, Stanley Salisbury, H. Cooper, George Bryan, H. Bingham Carre, T. Bennett, Oliver Gaunt, H. W. Parnacott, Gerald Goodridge, Cyril O'Keefe and Arthur Hill. I have also to acknowledge the kindness and advice accorded to me by Professor Gourlay and Mr. A. N. Paterson of Glasgow, Mr. Hippolyte J. Blanc of Edinburgh, Mr. R. M. Butler of Dublin, and Mr. Reay of Bath, all of whom received me with courtesy during my travels. I also much appreciate the enthusiasm of my assistants Messrs. Osmund Bellamy, Leopold Cole, Benson Greenall and T. Daniell, and Mr. Eric Wornum, who have spared no pains to furnish me with measured drawings and sketches and other help. I also wish to thank Mr. Percy J. Smith for designing the title-page. I must also record my indebtedness to the Council of the Royal Institute of British Architects for allowing the reproduction of certain drawings, and to the librarian, Mr. Rudolf Dircks, for his friendly comments; to the Authorities of the British Museum, and Mr. Strange, the keeper of the prints and drawings at South Kensington Museum, for granting special facilities for studying drawings and taking photographs. To the Governor of the Bank of England my thanks are due for the unique privilege accorded to my publishers to photograph, and for permission granted to me to study the whole of the Bank buildings; and to H.M. Office of Works for permission to measure several Government buildings. Lastly, my thanks are due to the Librarian of the Dublin Library, to the Librarian of the University Library, Cambridge, and to the Curator of the Fitzwilliam Museum, for courtesies shown to me.

A. E. R.

LIST OF PLATES

LIST OF PLATES

LIST OF PLATES

LIST OF TEXT ILLUSTRATIONS

LIST OF TEXT ILLUSTRATIONS

LIST OF TEXT ILLUSTRATIONS

CHAPTER I

INTRODUCTORY

There lies an antique region, on which fell
The dews of thought, in the world's golden dawn
Earliest and most benign; and from it sprung
Temples and cities and immortal forms,
And harmonies of wisdom and of song,
And thoughts, and deeds worthy of thoughts so fair.
And, when the sun of its dominion failed,
And when the winter of its glory came,
The winds that stripped it bare blew on, and swept
That dew into the utmost wildernesses
In wandering clouds of sunny rain that thawed
The unmaternal bosom of the North.

PERCY BYSSHE SHELLEY : *Herald of Eternity.*

AT the present time there is a growing appreciation for the academic phases of English Neo-Classic architecture; and more especially is attention being directed to the buildings conceived in the monumental manner.

The development of a distinct architectural style, from the time of Inigo Jones until late in the nineteenth century, not only produced great architectural triumphs, but in all its phases showed a tendency to return direct to the fountain-head of Classic inspiration—Greece and Rome. This tendency became clearly apparent at the beginning of the eighteenth century, and it was due in the main to the energies of the cultured amateurs who devoted both time and money for the extension of archæological research.

The first quarter of the eighteenth century marks the earliest period when the movement first bore definite results; henceforth, through the succeeding years, its growth was nourished by a continual stream of information concerning the antique, and by the study of a past art a living one was advanced. It reached its highest development in the hands of Professor Cockerell and Harvey Lonsdale Elmes, and eventually suffered temporary obscurity under the negative influences which characterised the last quarter of the nineteenth century. It is the object of the present volume to demonstrate the existence of the monumental in English architecture; and for this reason the minor issues of the remarkable Neo-Classic development in England are avoided as being controversial. Before summarising the various heads which mark the phases of the movement it will be necessary to give some explanation of the euphonious title " monumental."

The origin of monumental architecture is so indissolubly associated with the earliest attempts made by man to conventionalise the grandeur of Nature that, historically viewed, it appears to have been the office of Nature to educate in man a perception of the basic principles of architecture, as well as to inspire him with the desire to emulate her truths. Eternal, stimulating, and heroic in all her moods, she cast her spell with magic artistry over primitive man, compelling him to feast his eyes on splendid distances, inaccessible heights, and impressive depths. Against the azure dome of heaven she unrolled glorious compositions of clouds, and from the terrific contrasts depicted in her honest countenance man subconsciously drew his early inspirations. There is an affinity between Nature and noble architecture inasmuch as the latter is but a sequel to the original truths of Nature, the homage paid by man to her unfathomed secret. Architecture conceived in this spirit is best expressed by the term monumental because it embodies in its design a reflection of the physical harmonies. Not only does this æsthetic quality belong to the ideal aspect of design, but its principles are consonant with every aspect of the fine and mechanical arts.

I

MONUMENTAL ARCHITECTURE

Paramount among the earliest instances of monument-making stand the "rude stone monuments" of antiquity, the "cromlechs," "menhirs," and "tolmens" of Carnac and Stonehenge, the stupendous Pelasgian and Cyclopean remains, the rough circular enclosures devoted to ophiolatry, the rude cairns memorialising the dead, and the sacrificial and sepulchral stones found in every part of the world. Although these erections do not represent the origin of all architecture, yet all great architecture assimilates something of the spirit that hovers over such venerable structures.

There is in monumental architecture an indescribable austerity and remoteness, a sense of reposeful dignity, a solidity, steadiness, and simplicity of effect that impresses the mind at once with the greatness of the idea. The aspect of the great monuments of antiquity reveals the fact that in every case they possess the foregoing attributes, and that the same immutable idea permeates their design irrespective of nationality or period. Throughout the ages architects have endeavoured to recognise certain primary truths of design, building nobly with reticence and dignity to express a definite purpose.

There is ample evidence of the development of this theory to be seen in the ancient architecture of Egypt : the pyramids of Gizeh, the rock-cut tombs, the pylons and hypæthral courts of Thebes, Luxor, and Philæ bear eloquent witness to the ambitions of a departed race. The artificial plateaux and mounds of Babylonia, crowned by towers rising higher than the pyramids, the immensity of the ruined palaces of Persepolis, the dagobas and temples of India, all confirm the theory of the monumental manner. The buildings erected in those remote periods imparted to the art of architecture the character it has retained to the present day, and it is certain that the future will achieve no departure from the primal laws. From the instinct of monument-making arose the desire for noble architecture ; experience taught the value of order, rhythm, and proportion, and demonstrated how single units could be combined to form extended compositions.

Turning to the Hellenic world, we view the most important monument in the whole realm of architecture—the Athenian Parthenon. While the architecture of Hellas emanated from a different source from that whence sprung the architecture of Egypt and Assyria, it progressed to its culmination on almost parallel lines. In Crete, Sicily, Dorian Italy, Ionia, and the isles of the Archipelago were forged the links in the golden chain to be completed at Athens during the Periclean age. The design of the Greek temple in its compactness and completeness is expressive of the principles of abridgment and selection which are among the chief characteristics of Hellenistic architecture.

Rome, by her conquests, added to the indigenous Hellenistic forms, she imported Greek artificers to work her marbles, she secured the finest examples of Phidian sculpture to serve as models, and while outwardly professing the utmost contempt for the conquered Greeks herself fell vanquished before the Muse of Hellas.

The fusion of the Greek constructive principles with the system of arcuation formed the basis of Roman architecture, and an advance was made in the direction of comprehensive composition. This advance showed itself most clearly in the planning of the great public works, and buildings of diverse shapes and intended for different purposes were arranged to form incidents in schemes which were extensive and homogeneous, the *thermæ* of Caracalla, Diocletian, Nero, and Titus being examples of the practice of highly systematised methods of planning.

With the foundation of the Eastern Empire at Byzantium there concurred a return towards the finesse of Greek art which in a great measure reacted on the Romanesque architecture of Northern Italy and prepared the way for the revival of Classic thought in Europe. In Northern Europe arose the cathedrals of Notre Dame, Amiens, Chartres, and Beauvais in France ; Lincoln, Salisbury, and Durham in England. These monumental structures, dramatic in conception and glorious in the display of luxuriant detail, are commemorative of an epoch unprecedented in religious fervour.

The Italian Renaissance, in part a return towards the voluptuous life of the senses and the understanding, and in part a grand reaction against the mediæval sentiments of the heart and imagination, was productive of new and powerful forces. When we examine closely the various stages of this mighty movement, and study the palaces of Florence, Venice, and Rome, there is revealed in these convincing monuments the genesis of modern architecture. Notwithstanding the fact that the labours of the Italians were mainly directed toward a study of the antiquities in Italy,

INTRODUCTORY

there is ample evidence of their desire to pierce the veil of mystery which then enveloped Greece.

In the first period of the reawakening of Classical culture the great pioneer of the Renaissance, Poggio Bracciolini, had already obtained from Chios, in Greece, antiques to adorn his villa near Florence, the Valdarniana. Again, about the middle of the fifteenth century the enthusiastic traveller Cirioco de Pizzicolli of Ancona during his repeated wanderings through the islands of the Archipelago had turned his attention to the relics of Greek art. Baldassare Perruzi, working almost unnoticed, had also achieved a notable triumph by the near approach of his work to the technique of Greek architecture. The Italian masters Vignola and Palladio, in their attempt to systematise the proportions of the Classic orders by formulating rules, unconsciously effected the future proportioning of Classic architecture in France and England. By devious channels the flood-tide of the Renaissance beneficially found its way into other countries, irresistibly overpowering mediæval prejudices and gradually absorbing local traditions.

As early as the sixteenth century, in response to the appeal occasioned by the Renaissance, it was quite usual for Englishmen to go to Italy in pursuit of the higher culture. The flourishing universities of Bologna and Padua were regarded by British lovers of learning as the highest school, particularly for the students of law and medicine.

Among the foremost of the Englishmen to visit Italy was John Shute, who enjoyed the patronage of the Duke of Northumberland. Shute arrived at Rome in the year 1550, and studied under the best architects ; returning some years later, he published in 1563 the " First and Chief Groundes of Architecture."

Towards the close of the sixteenth century Inigo Jones visited Italy—the exact date is somewhat obscure ; and again between the years 1613–14, when he formed a member of the Earl of Arundel's *entourage*. He zealously studied the antiquities of Rome, making notes of the buildings, annotating his copy of " Palladio," and perfecting his knowledge of Classic architecture. He also collected works of art for the Earl of Arundel, the Earl of Pembroke, and Lord Danvers. During this visit the Earl of Arundel formed the nucleus of his famous collection of antique statuary, afterwards known as the Marmora Arundeliana, which was dispersed during the Commonwealth. The Duke of Buckingham also appears to have been a keen competitor for antique sculpture. It can also be attributed to the example of the Earl of Arundel and the Duke of Buckingham that King Charles I. likewise became a collector of antiques, and in 1628 took advantage of the presence in the Archipelago of his Admiral Sir Kenelm Digby to procure many remarkable specimens from those quarries.

The first quarter of the seventeenth century witnessed a change in the attitude of Englishmen towards architecture ; in place of a dumb acceptance of any architectural novelty there arose a desire among cultured men to inquire closely into the architecture of Italy *in situ*. At first the movement was scarcely perceptible, but it gradually gained ground, and these tentative visits to Italy and the shores of Greece presaged the more thorough archæological labours undertaken by Englishmen during the following century.

In the year 1619 Inigo Jones, in his capacity as Surveyor-General to the Works, was ordered to design the new Banqueting House at Whitehall in place of the old one, which had been destroyed by fire. He prepared a model of the building for the king's approval, and from start to finish its erection occupied three years. Considering the conditions of the period when this building was erected, its academic character is phenomenal. At that time it was without compeer, and, by comparison with such mansions as Burghley and Hatfield, the *naïveté* of the design appears heroic. The grandiose scheme prepared by Inigo Jones for the new palace at Whitehall, as well as the many Neo-Classic buildings accredited to John Webb, proclaim the efficacy of the Classic touchstone, the beginning of the monumental manner, which has survived to the present day.

The intervention of the Civil Wars checked alike the king's passion for antiquities and palaces. Architecture and the kindred arts suffered a temporary obscurity, only to be awakened to a greater refulgence by the genius of Sir Christopher Wren. The appearance in the architectural firmament of this particular star was opportune. All great movements, both historical and architectural, need

MONUMENTAL ARCHITECTURE

the concurrence of the man and the moment to bring them to a successful issue. The restoration of the monarchy and the Great Fire of London proved to be Wren's opportunity, and for sixty years he laboured incessantly to advance English architecture. As a monumental architect Wren ranks foremost amongst the giants; his City churches and St. Paul's Cathedral are unrivalled, not only for composition, but for the freshness and originality of their inspired conception. No

FIG. 1. THE MASTERPIECES OF SIR CHRISTOPHER WREN   *From a drawing by Professor C. R. Cockerell, R.A.*

greater tribute to the genius of the great architect could have been offered than Professor Cockerell's magnificent drawing, depicting the whole of Wren's buildings, with St. Paul's Cathedral as the fitting climax. It is evident that Wren worked under many disadvantages; he never visited Italy, and, with the exception of six months' stay in Paris, his experience of foreign travel was small.

In England during the seventeenth century details of antique architecture described in the English tongue were not readily obtainable. In 1663 there appeared Godfrey Richard's first translation of Palladio, and in 1664 John Evelyn, who had previously spent some years in foreign travel, published a translation of Freart's "Parallels," at the time considered a very important work. If the number of English books dealing with Classic architecture were few, there were many Italian and French volumes to take their place. Evelyn, who was Wren's great friend, probably brought to his notice such works as "Roma Antiquæ urbis splendor," by J. Laurus, published in 1612, and "Roma Antica e Moderna," by Franzini, published in 1643. In 1682 Antoine Desgodetz, who had previously spent sixteen months studying the ancient buildings in Rome, published his book "Les Edifices Antiques de Rome." This very accurate work contained numerous engravings of the ancient structures. Copies were brought to England, and the book appears to have been used for reference throughout the eighteenth century.

Wren was an ardent student of the teachings of Vitruvius, and within certain bounds tolerably conversant with good Roman detail. Of the refinement of Greek architecture he knew little, but it is safe to assume that a man of his artistic gifts would have spared no pains to master that complex

4

subject had the data been forthcoming. From the respective descriptions given by Vitruvius and Pliny he attempted conjectural restorations of the Temple of Diana at Ephesus and the Mausoleum at Halicarnassus. The effect of the latter essay in archæology became apparent when his pupil Hawksmoor erected the steeple of St. George's, Bloomsbury. Gradually the influence of Sir Christopher Wren's school waned, the spirit of research grew stronger, and the desire manifested on every side was for more precise and accurate information concerning Classic architecture. In consequence there followed a definite movement in favour of a higher standard of taste.

As early as the year 1674 Jacques Carrey, an artist who accompanied the Marquis de Nointel, French Ambassador to the Porte, had journeyed to Athens and made drawings of the sculptures of the Parthenon, prior to the destructive bombardment by the Venetians in 1687. This important visit to what at that time was an almost unknown land was followed by a tour of exploration undertaken by Mr. Vernon, Dr. Spon, and Sir George Wheler, who in 1676 visited the Acropolis and made notes on the ruins. It was not, however, until Stuart and Revett commenced their operations at Athens in the middle of the eighteenth century that attention was finally diverted from Italy to Greece.

At the beginning of the eighteenth century it came to be generally realised that "the Grand Tour" through the Continental countries, particularly France and Italy, was a necessary complement to the education of a gentleman, and that artistic taste was an essential element. Foremost among the distinguished men who initiated the fashion of "the Grand Tour" stand the names of Sir Andrew Fountaine and Richard Boyle, Earl of Burlington. Mr. Thomas Coke, afterwards Earl of Leicester, was a younger contemporary of Lord Burlington, and no less energetic as a collector. The main object of the amateurs seems to have been to acquire objects of art; antique statues, vases, and pictures were imported to England, and in many cases the acquisition of such treasures provided the excuse for building new mansions.

Noblemen often employed their architects to act as their agents to buy antiquities; the architects were thus brought into immediate contact with Classic architecture at first hand. Under the patronage of the Earl of Burlington there occurred a hardening of the vernacular style, a definite trend towards the correctness of Palladio's work, which was further enriched by a direct study of the Roman ruins. Then followed a Roman Palladian phase of English Classic architecture, which lasted throughout the eighteenth century. The attention of architects was thereby directed, not only to the minor differences in the detail of the architectural orders, but to something of vastly greater importance—the appreciation of monumental qualities. Herein is to be seen the first indication of an academic style, displacing the provincial style heretofore the vogue. The establishment by the French Government of the Grand Prix de Rome in the year 1720 for the benefit of French students is the next point for consideration, because here too is apparent an important factor in the development of monumental architecture. The French were the first to foresee the advantages that would accrue to the art of architecture by the formation of an academy. They possess to a very considerable degree an instinct for what is right and wrong in architectural matters; as a result there is to be seen in French architecture a remarkable consistency, a levelling up in favour of a general idea rather than an encouragement of haphazard individuality. Briefly, this is what is meant by the term academic as applied to architecture.

On the other hand, the provincial spirit is apt to over-estimate the value of its ideas for want of a high standard by which to examine them. Evidence of this fault is apparent in the design of the Elizabethan and Jacobean mansions. Such structures represent no great architectural idea; they rely for their dominant expression on a display of adventitious ornament, borrowed in many cases from obscure sources without inquiry. The provincial spirit, for want of controlling criticism, gives one idea too much prominence at the expense of others. Its ideas, however brilliant, are arranged promiscuously, its fancies are too varied, its likes and dislikes are disproportionate.

Owing to the lack of a controlling intelligence the provincial in architecture has not urbanity, it does not rise to the intellectual tone of the capital. To emancipate architecture from provinciality is an important stage of culture; failing this the desired platform is never reached where alone the highest work begins. When the work of architects reaches this platform it becomes Classical, and it is the only work which can stand the test of time and secure the approbation of future ages. The less architecture comes within the influence of a centre of correct information, sound criticism, and good taste, the more discernible will be the note of provinciality. Any style that is remote in effect from the charm of acknowledged models or divergent from Classic truth and grace must surely fall within the definition of the term provincial. Mediæval Gothic architecture is within its own sphere eminently academic. The great cathedrals set the standard of taste ; the abbeys and parish churches and smaller buildings are in sympathetic consonance.

Previous to the eighteenth century, with its return to the Classic models of Italy and Greece, with the exception of the buildings designed by Inigo Jones and Sir Christopher Wren, the majority of English Neo-Classic buildings were provincial, starting with those which displayed an illiterate smattering of applied architectural orders and inconsequent strap-work, characteristic of the Elizabethan age, and continuing with those exhibiting coarse detail and crude ornament purporting to be Classic.

The monumental manner in architecture is so closely allied to the academic style as to be indivisible. It impresses the mind at once with one great idea ; it is rarely found in architecture merely picturesque or respected solely for its historic associations, neither does it rely for its effect on elegant ornamentation.

In basing the modern development of monumental architecture on the matured style of Greece and Rome the architects of the eighteenth century showed great foresight. To quote Sir Joshua Reynolds, " The fire of the artist's own genius operating upon these materials which have been thus diligently collected will enable him to make new combinations, perhaps superior to what had ever been before in the possession of the art, as in the mixture of the variety of metals, which are said to have been melted and run together at the burning of Corinth, a new and till then unknown metal was produced, equal in value to any of those that had contributed to its composition."

The coterie of eighteenth-century architects who laboured for the development of a correct architectural style had the inestimable advantage of an appreciative audience. The amateur assisted the architect in every possible way ; not only did he take architects under his patronage and shape their studies by sending them to Rome, but he provided the necessary funds for archæological research. The foundation of the Society of Dilettanti in the year 1734 is ample proof of the deep artistic interest that existed amongst gentlemen of culture. The publication of Wood and Dawkins' two volumes in the years 1753–57, illustrating the ruins of Baalbec and Palmyra, directed the attention of architects and others to the vast extent and magnificence of Roman colonial architecture. But the value of these volumes was completely overshadowed by Stuart and Revett's " Classical Antiquities of Athens," the first volumes of which appeared in 1762. In connection with this work, which well merited the success it received, it must be understood that its issue was anticipated by three years, owing to the publication of a rival book compiled by the Frenchman M. Le Roy. Supported by royal favour and private interest, Le Roy reached Athens in 1753 ; and on his return he published an account of his researches, illustrated with plates ; an English translation, also illustrated, was brought out by Robert Sayer in 1759. Parallel with the production of illustrated books describing the architecture of Greece there appeared others dealing with the architecture of Rome, the most important being Robert Adam's " Ruins of Diocletian's Palace at Spalatro," published in 1764, and the " Architectural Antiquities of Rome," by Taylor and Cresy, published in two volumes as late as the years 1821–22.

The buildings erected from the year 1730 onwards reflect the rigid architectural discipline of the age. Composition on an extensive scale became the mode, improvements in planning and refinement in detail distinguished the work of the period from the imperfections of the style which preceded it.

It must be universally acknowledged that the works of James Gibbs, Richard Cassells, John Carr, Sir Robert Taylor, Sir William Chambers, the brothers Adam, James Gandon, and George Dance the younger afford a rich collection of buildings conceived in the monumental manner.

INTRODUCTORY

In the polished style of Sir William Chambers, as in the vigorous manner of George Dance the younger, will be found qualities both imaginative and scholarly.

Progressing from the early phases of the academic style as developed by Richard Cassells, John Carr, and Sir Robert Taylor, there is to be seen in the buildings designed by Chambers, Gandon, and the brothers Adam a slight affectation of the prevalent French manner—namely, the style Louis Seize. Even James Stuart, fresh from his explorations in Greece, was forced to acknowledge the existing traditions, and only succeeded in blending the refinements of Greek detail with the features of the vernacular style. The triumph of the Roman Palladian school, however, must be accorded to George Dance the younger, whose design for Newgate Prison created one of the most imaginative monumental structures in the whole history of English architecture.

In connection with the succeeding phase it would be difficult to determine precisely where the Græco-Roman school began, so thoroughly does it interlock and overlap with the preceding period. Henry Holland claimed to have originated the new movement, a distinction which indubitably belongs by right to James Stuart, who was not only the pioneer of Greek research, but had erected No. 15 St. James's Square for Lord Anson some time before Holland started in practice as an architect.

Passing over the names of S. P. Cockerell, Thomas Harrison, and the Wyatts, all of whom produced buildings belonging to the Græco-Roman school, the work of Sir John Soane marks another stage. Emanating from the office of Dance, and spending some time with Henry Holland, Soane was nurtured amidst Classic traditions. He also obtained a sound training in the schools of the Royal Academy, with a period of three years' foreign study in Italy. In the more important of his architectural works, eminently scholarly as they are, there is revealed a strange variety of cross-purposes. Soane never seems to have understood the value of the dictum that " True art is to conceal art." In the design of his academic compositions his art is too apparent. His versatile mind could not remain satisfied with the urbanity of simple dignity, for his facile pencil continually led him to strive after undue originality. Nearly all his preliminary designs and sketches reveal the same characteristic ; there is always present some idiosyncrasy which added nothing to the academic aspect of his work. In spite of these faults he lacked neither imagination nor enterprise ; he had a profound knowledge of Classic architecture, and great ability in the handling of complex problems of planning.

The much-abused John Nash seems to have taken an entirely different view of the monumental manner. Compared with Sir John Soane, who could never be sure as to the form subsidiary features should take, Nash neglected detail in preference for breadth of treatment. The town-planning schemes of the Regency were mainly the outcome of his energies ; and whatever may be urged condemnatory of the detail and construction of his buildings, they were always conceived in an academic spirit. Nash was a master of comprehensive street design. Like Sir John Vanbrugh, he treated his ranges of buildings in the manner of a scene-painter. Each group of the buildings in Regent Street and Regent's Park supports another in massing. They are entirely dissimilar in their individual grouping, yet their resulting unification is as refreshing as it is rare. Apart from the insincerity and the theatric display governing the terraces of Regent's Park or the stuccoed squares of Belgravia, there is something intrinsically human in the scale of these masses of conventional scenery. Carlyle raved against them as being acrid putrescences, but he failed to appreciate the academic tone their design imparts to the West End of London. The monumental manner primarily relies on uniformity for its impressiveness. Better by far the architecture of Regent Street as first created by John Nash than the ragged confusion which at present desolates many of London's principal streets.

The first quarter of the nineteenth century was on the whole distinguished by the peculiarly lively interest taken by the public and architects alike in pure Greek architecture. The Græco-Roman school was gradually merged into a Greek phase, the outcome of the archæological researches, at that time confined almost entirely to Greece. Its chief exponents in England were William Wilkins, Gandy-Deering, Sir Robert Smirke, Decimus Burton, and the Inwoods, while the Scotch group consisted of Archibald Elliot, Thomas Hamilton, William Playfair, and William

MONUMENTAL ARCHITECTURE

Burn. Transitionary as the Greek phase eventually proved, it nevertheless marked an important advance towards the culminating stage of the movement.

We cannot entirely refuse to Sir Robert Smirke the wreath of approbation. He was a monumentalist in the fullest sense of the word at a time when other men were trifling with Gothic architecture. His deficiency lay in the fact that he did not possess the power to impart warmth of character to his creations. The main front of the British Museum is an example of this deficiency. Thomas Hamilton, however, in his notable building, the High School at Edinburgh, evolved one of the most superb modern structures inspired by Athenian models. In this building Hamilton ordered his masses like a giant, arranging them as an integral part of the cognate rock which forms their setting, and employing a subtle curved frontage line to embody the whole grouping.

The chief fault of the Greek school—and it must be frankly admitted—consists of a too literal reproduction of naked Greek forms without due regard to the essential accessory features of ornament and sculpture.

The full force of the rage created by Stuart and Revett's pioneer labours in the Classic fields of Greece had in the course of fifty years spread over Europe. Architects and antiquaries of all nationalities journeyed to Greece, with the result that archæological research assumed the scientific form it holds to-day. Englishmen more especially may well experience satisfaction and pride as they review the long list of distinguished and respected names of men who devoted years of labour to the noble advancement of taste.

The most brilliant phase in the history of the monumental manner is to be seen in the Neo-Grec and Italian culmination. Here too came the reaction which follows on the heels of every excess. The leaders of architectural thought were the first to revolt against the indiscriminate reproduction of Greek temples which had hitherto obsessed some minds ; they realised that a counter-action was necessary to check the prosaic copyism of old Classic art. In consequence a determined and sustained effort was made to arrest the stagnation of creative impulse, as well as to turn the arts of design from the species of *cul-de-sac* towards which they were drifting.

The preceding phase of the academic style had, in spite of the fashionable affectation of Greek forms, not only brought about a renewed love for joyous Greek architecture, but also an awakening to a fuller sense of its original beauty. There followed a broad-minded movement in favour of eclecticism, essentially modern in sentiment and directed towards a study of every phase of Classic art.

About the year 1830 a modified style of design, since termed Neo-Grec, was introduced by the far-seeing efforts of a number of European architects. Its development profoundly affected the practice of Classic architecture in the direction of freedom and refinement. In France, where the Neo-Grec movement first came into being, Duc, Duban, and Labrouste were its most active spirits. In England Professor C. R. Cockerell, Harvey Lonsdale Elmes, Sir Charles Barry, and Sir James Pennethorne, during their distinguished careers, demonstrated the suitability of Classic art to the exigencies of modern civilisation. In Germany the masterly conceptions of Karl Friedrich Schinkel, Leo von Klenze, Stüler, and Châteauneuf testify to the cosmopolitan character the development assumed.

The explanation of the crude-sounding term Neo-Grec means, in a literal sense, fresh Greek. Its essence is finesse. The *motifs* of the Neo-Grec phase were selected, derived from, or inspired by the old Greek, the old Roman, or the Italian Renaissance. Having reached a certain stage in the development of an academic style, the artists went back for fresh material, to begin again with the first elements on the most advanced stage.

This method of procedure is strikingly illustrated in the buildings designed by Professor Cockerell. His early impressions of architectural form were gathered during the time he spent in the office of his father, who then was one of the chief exponents of the Græco-Roman school, and later in the office of Sir Robert Smirke he experienced that architect's predilections for pure Greek. As a student Cockerell entertained great respect for the works of Sir Christopher Wren ; therefore it is apparent that his knowledge of architecture was considerable, even before he had the advantage of

INTRODUCTORY

foreign travel. An archæologist of the first rank, Cockerell knew the limitations archæology imposed on creative impulse, especially if a vain display of learning were persisted in. Deeply versed as he was in the knowledge of Hellenic art, he forbore the interpretation of its forms in any spirit other than that of freedom. He was eminently modern in the catholicity of his tastes, he carried the excellences of Sir Christopher Wren's buildings back to meet the Italian *motif*, and infused them with the true Promethean fire of old Greece and Rome.

While Cockerell was still at some distance from the zenith of his career a young and unknown man came into dazzling prominence as the author of the winning design for St. George's Hall at Liverpool. The pathetically short career of Harvey Lonsdale Elmes contributed to English Neo-Classic a building coequal in merit with St. Paul's Cathedral, a structure, moreover, unlike any other that had previously existed, and one which by reason of its monumental qualities forms the fitting climax to a great movement.

Contemporary with the Neo-Grec phase, additional impetus was given to the use of the Italian astylar *motif* by Sir Charles Barry's design for the Travellers' Club, which he followed at a later date by the Reform Club and Bridgewater House. Dorchester House, Park Lane, designed by Vulliamy, and several of the large blocks of terraces facing Kensington Gardens, show this influence. Barry enjoyed one of the largest practices of his day, and throughout his valuable career his tastes were always on the Classic side. The Houses of Parliament in their composition and planning arrangements display a Classic feeling, and in spite of Pugin's Gothic dressing, magnificent as it is, there is revealed the handling of a Classicist.

After the death of Cockerell in 1863 the Gothic school gained the ascendancy in the tastes of the public. Sir James Pennethorne, Frederick Pepys Cockerell, and Alexander Thomson were the last of the coterie who laboured to keep the Classic lamp from being entirely extinguished. Lord Palmerston's insistence for a Classic design when the new Home Office buildings were contemplated resulted in the ineffective battle of the styles, from which neither side emerged with added dignity. But the approval of the Government having once been given to the continuance of Classic architecture, there followed the masterly designs by James Williams for the new Post Office buildings in Newgate Street, Queen Victoria Street, and at Manchester.

The history of English architecture from the year 1870 until within the last decade consists of a series of attempts to revive the various styles, each more or less provincial in their handling. For a time the academic aspect of Classic architecture has been partially interpreted, its truths have suffered censure as being ephemeral and fallacious. Yet the monumental in architecture, as in Nature, is universal, it is eternal, and it is true.

In the succeeding chapters of this volume will be found a full analysis of the various stages of the development, which, for the purpose of emphasising the career of each individual architect in relation to the whole movement, has been arranged in biographical form.

The phases of the monumental manner are divided into four main groups, the date limits assigned being wholly arbitrary, since at no time did there exist any definite division between them. but always the guiding identity of the themes of antiquity, which are in essence a crystallisation of Nature's truths.

CHAPTER II

THE ROMAN PALLADIAN PHASE, 1730–1780

THE EARL OF BURLINGTON—RICHARD CASSELLS—GIACOMO LEONI—
GEORGE DANCE THE ELDER—JOHN WOOD OF BATH—SIR ROBERT
TAYLOR—JOHN CARR OF YORK—THE BROTHERS ADAM—THOMAS
SANDBY—SIR WILLIAM CHAMBERS—JAMES GANDON—THOMAS COOLEY—
GEORGE DANCE THE YOUNGER

AT the beginning of the eighteenth century no other European country with the exception of France, the forcing-ground of culture, could boast an aristocracy so keenly interested in Classic art as were the English nobility. The intense enthusiasm displayed at this period had in the main been generated during the early years of the previous century, when the tentative visits of Englishmen to Italy had first opened the sealed book of Classic architecture to British eyes. A new era in architectural design was beginning, precise and scholarly in its tendencies, but one which owed its very essence to the pioneer labours of the two great English architects, Inigo Jones and Sir Christopher Wren. The romantic seventeenth century had provided many opportunities for architectural genius ; even the civil wars did not completely overshadow the brilliancy of the Classic torch kindled by Inigo Jones, and when Sir Christopher Wren came into prominence after the Great Fire, as architect for St. Paul's Cathedral and the City churches, interest in architecture became widespread. It was not, however, until the establishment of George I. on the throne, with his court of German retainers, and Addison as Secretary of State, that polite society became enamoured of the fashion of the Grand Tour, undertaken through the Continental countries, and particularly France and Italy. Although the influence of Sir Christopher Wren and his school became less apparent at this period, his contemporaries and successors were forced to acknowledge the truths of his principles, and, moreover, continued to practise them in their own work. In this regard the work of John Vanbrugh, particularly Blenheim and Castle Howard, serves to connect the school of Sir Christopher Wren with that evolved under the *ægis* of the Earl of Burlington.

The curious age of dilettantism coincided with the reign of George I., when Pope and Swift and Bolingbroke yet lived and wrote, when a society vast in numbers and brilliant in culture dominated the court, patronised artists, and posed as oracles in matters of good taste. By a study of the architecture of that day we may peep into the bygone conditions of English life, note the new influences which were brought to bear on the vernacular style, and discern through it all the genius of the English race asserting itself in terms of reticent and austere architecture.

The academic in art was sought for and appreciated at its proper value ; Rome became the academy not only for the wealthy nobleman, but for the young artist seeking both knowledge and patronage. In consequence of the increasing number of English visitors to Italy, and the acquisition of antiquities by these distinguished travellers, there was published in the year 1722 the first English guide to the works of art in Italy, a very accurate volume compiled by Jonathan Richardson and his son.

Foremost among the English noblemen who did most to raise architecture to the academic platform stands the name of Richard Boyle, Earl of Burlington and Cork. He brought Giacomo Leoni to England to superintend the English edition of Palladio which appeared in 1717, and through his liberality "Robert Castells's Villas of the Ancients" was published in 1728. He purchased in Italy the original drawings showing the restoration of the Roman Thermæ, and published them in 1730 under the title of "Fabbriche Antiche disegnate da Andrea Palladio." He was also the patron of William Kent, Brettingham the elder, and Colin Campbell. The Earl of Burlington and his school, while they accepted the teachings of Palladio, held in reverence the

FIG. 2. THE PARLIAMENT HOUSE, DUBLIN, 1730-39   *Richard Cassells, Architect*

glories of old Rome ; but at the time the works of the Italian master provided a more ready model on which to base the new movement, which resulted in the Palladian phase of the monumental manner. The noble Earl was a man of considerable discrimination in matters of taste, and exercised great influence over the men he patronised, but no record of his personal prowess as an architect is forthcoming.

The first building of importance to show the new influence was the Parliament House in Dublin, built between the years 1730–39. This structure was noted at the time of its erection, as it is now, for the simplicity of its composition and the refinement of its detail. Richard Cassells is asserted to have been the architect, although some doubt exists as to how far he was responsible for the design. Harris, writing in 1766, mentions that the building was erected under the inspection of Sir Edward Lovett Pearce and Arthur Dobbs, at a cost of £40,000. In 1785 Gandon added the circular east wing, as well as the Corinthian portico forming the main entrance to the House of Lords ; and between the years 1792–94 the west portico and circular colonnade were erected by Robert Parke,

FIG. 3. THE PARLIAMENT HOUSE, DUBLIN. THE WEST PORTICO AND CIRCULAR COLONNADE, 1792–94   *Robert Parke, Architect*

who remodelled Gandon's circular east wing to accord with the main portion of the original building.

Further extensive alterations were eventually carried out by Francis Johnston. The main feature of

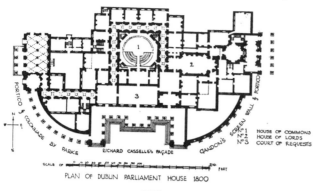

FIG. 4.

PLAN OF DUBLIN PARLIAMENT HOUSE 1800

the building, namely, the House of Commons, was originally roofed by a dome, modelled upon that of the Pantheon at Rome, and, considering the date of its erection, was an accomplished piece of Classic design.

Another building of the same period, exhibiting refining influences, is the house now known as Nos. 57 and 58 Lincoln's Inn Fields, built in 1735, probably from a design by Giacomo Leoni.

Broadly speaking, the number of public buildings erected in Great Britain between the years 1730–60 were comparatively few; on this account the ambitions of the architects were limited to the design of town and country mansions for the nobility and other members of society. To this period belongs the group of mansions designed by John Vardy, Isaac Ware, James Paine, John Carr of York, and Sir Robert Taylor. All the latter buildings reflect the steadying influence of

FIG. 5. THE PARLIAMENT HOUSE, DUBLIN. INTERIOR VIEW

Richard Cassells, Architect

the Classical spirit. Another prominent architect of the day was George Dance the elder; he was appointed Clerk of the City Works in 1733, and in 1739 designed the Mansion House, which he completed in 1753. In 1740 William Jones, who was surveyor of the East India Company, built the Rotunda at Ranelagh, a building representing an adaptation of the Pantheon at Rome. Another early instance of a Classic prototype being followed was evidenced when John Wood remodelled the city of Bath; there he extended the principle of composing several buildings into one comprehensive scheme, an idea which had been previously demonstrated by Inigo Jones. The Royal Circus is an example of Wood's study of superimposed orders, adapted to modern purposes.

In all the above-mentioned works there is apparent a great advance in the arrangement of the constituent masses of architectural compositions, as compared with the achievements of the preceding school. Even John Vanbrugh, with his imaginative genius for great conceptions and obsession for Titanic structures, lost sight of the golden rule of simplicity in design, and by introducing a multiplicity of features, as at Blenheim and Castle Howard, sacrificed dignity of effect to a gorgeously picturesque silhouette.

His work forms an interesting link between the teachings of Sir Christopher Wren's vernacular

Plate I.

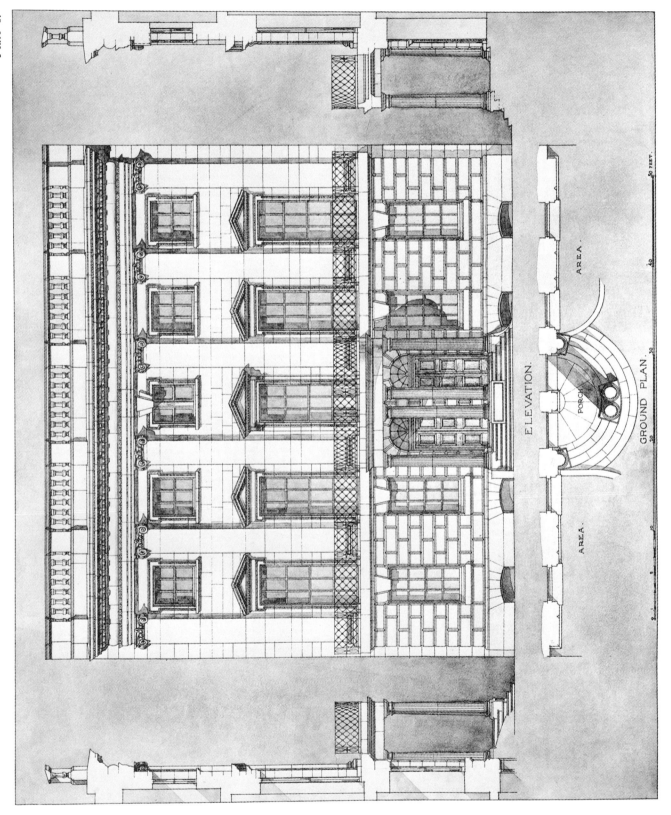

ELEVATION.

AREA.

AREA.

PORCH

GROUND PLAN.

50 FEET.

Nos. 57, 58 LINCOLNS INN FIELDS, LONDON.

THE CIRCULAR PORCH ADDED BY SIR JOHN SOANE. PROBABLY DESIGNED BY LEONI, 1735.

style, and the more studied acceptance of Palladio's doctrines, whereas the details of Vanbrugh's buildings reveal a serious tendency to repeat the disciplined elements, inherent in contemporary French architecture, the style Louis Quatorze. Such works as those of James Gibbs, particularly the magnificent exterior to the Radclyffe Library at Oxford, while retaining the vigorous manner engendered by the labours of Sir Christopher Wren, show the hand of the barometer setting fair for academic refinement.

FIG. 6. THE MANSION HOUSE, LONDON. *George Dance the elder, Architect*

Further evidence of the increase of the Palladian influence is offered by George Dance's original design for the Mansion House. This structure

FIG. 7. THE ROYAL CIRCUS, BATH *John Wood, Architect*

MONUMENTAL ARCHITECTURE

formerly carried twin storeys above the attic storey, about which much criticism raged ; but at that period the official residence of the chief magistrate formed the most prominent building in the city, and it was evidently Dance's idea to emphasise the fact. Although the design and proportion of these features were exaggerated, their removal leaves something lacking in the aspect of the building.

The Woods of Bath, father and son, although removed at a great distance from other cultured exponents in London, raised the standard of architecture in the West of England, and ineffaceably left their seal on the facial aspect of Bath. John Wood built Prior Park for Ralph Allen ; later he carried out the Exchange at Bristol, and the Town Hall and Exchange at Liverpool, the latter was demolished fifty years ago.

The purely architectural qualities displayed in the work of these talented men incontestably proves the advantages which accrued to the practice of architecture at that period, by reason of the increase of travel and knowledge of the antique.

The next architect of importance to be considered is Sir Robert Taylor (1714–88). His monumental works include Stone Buildings, Lincoln's Inn, built in 1756, the addition of the two wings on either side of Sampson's original façade at the Bank of England, and numerous internal works for that building which he carried out between the years 1766–71–83. In 1775 the "six Clerks and Enrolment Office" in Chancery Lane and the old Patent Office in Quality Court were probably designed by him.

FIG. 8. THE OLD PATENT OFFICE, QUALITY COURT, CHANCERY LANE. Built 1760. Demolished 1901

Sir Robert Taylor, Architect

Sir Robert Taylor had travelled in Italy during the early years of his career, and on his return to England followed the vocation of a sculptor ; the pediment of the Mansion House is an example of his skill in that capacity. From the standpoint of monumental design his important architectural works were in marked contrast to those of many of his contemporaries, being distinguished by simplicity of composition and almost Spartan severity in the selection of the enrichments.

Although the reputation of James Paine primarily rests upon his designs for country mansions, he is fully entitled, nevertheless, to recognition as an exponent of the monumental manner. His scheme for Kedleston Hall shows the handling of one well versed in classic composition, and although this structure was finally completed by the Brothers Adam the credit of the design belongs to Paine.

Among other important structures, he designed Richmond Bridge and bridges at Chertsey, Walton, and Kew.

John Carr of York (1723–1807) was a contemporary of Sir Robert Taylor, the County

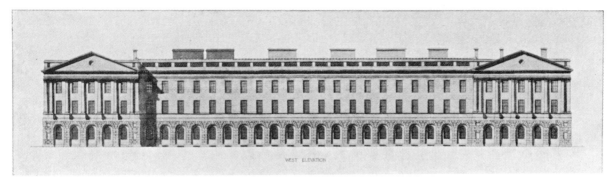

WEST ELEVATION

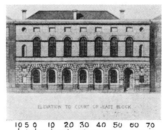

FIG. 9. STONE BUILDINGS, LINCOLN'S INN (1756)

ELEVATION TO COURT OF EAST BLOCK

Sir Robert Taylor, Architect

10 5 0   10   20 30 40 50 60 70
SCALE OF FEET

Court House at York, built between the years 1765–77, being his chief public work in the style.

His career is somewhat analogous to that of James Paine and Sir Robert Taylor. All three were in practice at the middle of the eighteenth century, and their work foreshadowed, if it did not materially aid, the trend of thought pursued by Chambers and the Brothers Adam.

In addition to the Court House, he built the Castle and the Gaol at York, a town hall at Newark,

FIG. 10. THE COURT HOUSE, YORK (1765)

John Carr, Architect

and the graceful crescent at Buxton. The last-named place was just becoming fashionable as a spa. But his main energies were engaged in the direction of domestic architecture, and such mansions as Lytham Hall in Lancashire, Basildon Park, Berkshire, and Dunton Park were designed and carried into being. He also designed the Mausoleum at Wentworth, and a bridge over the Wye at

Boroughbridge. In regard to the design of private palaces the composition of Harewood House, Yorkshire, stands out in well-defined prominence, especially the design of the southern front. The latter consists of a composition of three masses connected by means of links at a lower level, relieved by a dignified treatment of projecting steps and lengthy terracing.

The Court House at York, although far from being the largest building he evolved, is certainly the most interesting from

FIG. 11. THE ADMIRALTY SCREEN, WHITEHALL, BEFORE THE ALTERATIONS
Robert Adam, Architect

an academic standpoint. The proportions of the main façade are scholarly, the composition of the three masses is well considered, and the detail is delicate and refined without being effeminate, and moreover the character and purpose of the structure is unmistakable. Carr's various attainments, in nearly every instance, were free from such idiosyncrasies as gigantic keystones, absurd rustications, and other redundancies. He kept his individual manner within the bounds of the growing tradition, and he was well content to be governed by considerations of good taste. Although comparisons are impertinent, Carr's works, when considered in regard to those evolved by

such a master as Sir William Chambers, do not quite reach the high level attained by his brilliant young contemporary. In the minor works of Chambers, as well as in the works of Gandon, evidence of the strong hold Palladianism had gained at this period is apparent.

It was not, however, until after the first half of the eighteenth century had been reached that the archæological researches undertaken by Englishmen began

FIG. 12. THE ADMIRALTY SCREEN WITH COLUMNS REMOVED   *Robert Adam, Architect*   to influence taste by

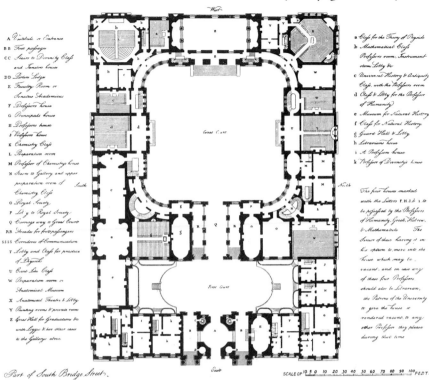

FIG. 13. EDINBURGH UNIVERSITY PLAN

means of the folio publications. In 1753 Wood and Dawkins's "Ruins of Palmyra" was published, followed, some time after, by "Ruins of Baalbec." Both these volumes directed attention to the great temple enclosures of the East, and at the time of their issue they aroused widespread interest, more especially toward the Roman methods of planning. About this date, 1754, the brilliant Scotsman Robert Adam (1728–92), accompanied by the young French draughtsman Clerisseau, visited Italy. Their tour eventually extended to Spalato, where they spent five weeks measuring and sketching the ruined palace of Diocletian. A folio volume containing the result of their work was published in 1764. Robert Adam returned to England in 1758, his first monumental work being the Admiralty Screen, erected about 1760. In 1775, with his brother James, he designed Drury Lane Theatre, and between the years 1778–87 the energies of the brothers were concentrated on the design of Edinburgh University. It is somewhat remarkable that, with the exception of the Admiralty Screen, the main portion of the Edinburgh University, and the New Assembly Rooms at Glasgow, the work of the Adams seldom attained to monumental dignity. The redoubtable brothers were masters of the formal methods of town-planning, and enriched both Edinburgh and London by their untiring labours. In London Portland Place, Stratford Place, the Adelphi, and Fitzroy Square are the most notable examples of their skill in comprehensive street design. Their individual designs were always cohesive in principle, and their finished works are models of

FIG. 14. EDINBURGH UNIVERSITY   *Robert and James Adam, Architects*

MONUMENTAL ARCHITECTURE

FIG. 15. THE HALL OF THE FREEMASONS' TAVERN, GREAT QUEEN STREET, LONDON,
AS ORIGINALLY EXISTING

From a Drawing in the Soane Collection   *Thomas Sandby, Architect*

texture values, especially in regard to the treatment of stone surfaces. They seldom rightly adapted the orders, and in many instances these features, when employed in their designs, are deficient in impressiveness. When the first volume of Stuart and Revett's "Antiquities of Athens" was published in 1762, the brothers Adam eagerly accepted the fresh ornamental *motifs* contained therein, which they cleverly embodied in their designs for decoration. The success of their own style is mainly attributable to their ability for imparting a character of rich refinement to their works, which secured for them extensive patronage and ensured the popularity of their designs. In brief, they belonged to the ornamental rather than to the monumental school, sacrificing grandeur of conception to an elegant mannerism.

Piranesi's etchings were also of importance to the development of the monumental manner, inasmuch as they directed the attention of architects to the glories of Rome. In 1748 appeared " Opere Varie," containing twenty-nine plates, and in 1750 " Le Carceri d'Invenzione." Subsequent works were issued in 1760, 1762, 1769, and 1778. Throughout the second half of the eighteenth century, as well as during the first portion of the nineteenth, these plates were held in high esteem by English architects, who referred to them for inspiration in design, and it was exceptional for an architect to be without some volumes in his library.

The establishment of the Royal Academy in 1768 stimulated architecture and the kindred arts to an unprecedented extent. The brilliant discourses of Sir Joshua Reynolds, together with the knowledge that royal patronage was extended to embrace the arts, acted as a spur to the young artists of the time. Thomas Sandby, born in 1721, was appointed the first professor of architecture to the Royal Academy Schools. His most important architectural work was the hall of the Freemasons' Tavern in Great Queen Street, built in 1775 and pulled down in 1864, an original drawing of which is now exhibited in the Diploma Gallery of the Royal Academy. He also prepared a design for a triumphal bridge based on a conception by Piranesi ; this formed part

18

Plate II.

SOMERSET HOUSE, LONDON. RIVER FRONT.

SIR WILLIAM CHAMBERS, ARCHITECT 1776. COMPLETED BY SIR ROBERT SMIRKE AND SIR JAMES PENNETHORNE.

Plate III.

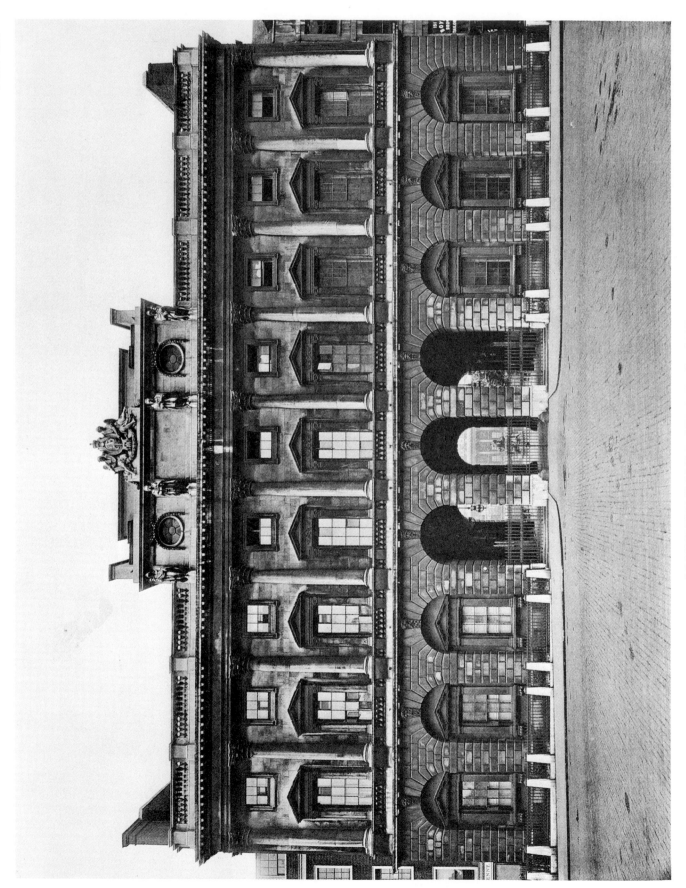

SOMERSET HOUSE, STRAND FRONT.
SIR WILLIAM CHAMBERS, ARCHITECT, 1776.

of a scheme for a royal palace at Westminster.* Sandby held the same views concerning architecture as his friend Sir William Chambers, and in his capacity as professor assisted many a young architect of the day to formulate his studies on sound academic principles.

When Sir William Chambers returned to England from China in 1742 he resolved to seriously take up architecture as a profession, and with this idea he studied drawing in Paris under Clerisseau, who was only a few years his senior. These early labours in Paris were augmented by a long stay in Italy, where he made studies of the buildings and writings of Michael Angelo, Vignola, Palladio, Scammozi, and Bernini. It is apparent from his subsequent achievements that his early impressions of architectural composition, obtained from the contemporary structures then progressing in Paris,

FIG. 16. ROYAL BANK OF SCOTLAND, ST. ANDREW'S SQUARE, EDINBURGH
Sir William Chambers, Architect

were intensified by his tour in Italy. Beginning active practice, Chambers brought to bear on the vernacular style a predilection for the contemporary French version of the antique. This explains the similitude in detail which exists between Somerset House, the Marino at Clontarf, and other of his works, and the works of Servandony, Soufflot, Neufforge, and Gabriel. The palaces fronting the old Place Louis XV. (now the Place de la Concorde) were being built between the years 1761–70, some years before the rebuilding of Somerset House was mooted, and the designs were known to Chambers, who appreciated the elegant French detail, more especially the exterior enrichments, which he followed as a *motif* on several occasions. This similarity in the selection of ornament is noticeable more particularly in the detail of the doors to the great courtyard at Somerset House, which recall those at the Hôtel des Monnaies, Paris, built between the years 1771–75 by Jacques Denis Antoine. Chambers's architectural sympathies were mainly Roman, and during the early stages of his career he designed several small casinos or temples to meet the fashion of the day. Among these were those at Wilton, Tanfield Hall, Wanstead, and that at Clontarf, built for Lord Charlemont, which it is rumoured cost £60,000. Lord Charlemont's house in Dublin is said to be the joint product of his lordship and Sir William Chambers; however, the refining hand of Chambers is more than discernible. About this time he was engaged on the erection of the theatre and chapel in Trinity College, which were carried out by his pupil Meyers. The façade to College Green was erected from a design given by Keane and Saunderson. While engaged in Scotland building Duddingstone House, near Edinburgh, he erected in the year 1768, for Sir L. Dundas, the building in St. Andrew's Square which is now used for the Royal Bank of Scotland.

The rebuilding of Old Somerset House in 1776 was his great opportunity to erect a monumental structure. Chambers enjoyed considerable influence in Court circles, and this secured him the appointment. A scheme had previously been prepared by Mr. Robinson, secretary to the Board of Works, for barracks and Government offices on the site of the Savoy; on the death of Robinson these plans were handed over to Chambers, who discarded them as useless. The pulling down of the old palace and the erection of the new building proceeded simultaneously; during the progress of the works Chambers was subjected to severe criticism, and needed all the help he could obtain

* A copy of this drawing is in the Soane Collection.

MONUMENTAL ARCHITECTURE

FIG. 17. SOMERSET HOUSE AND WATERLOO BRIDGE, SHOWING GENERAL COMPOSITION

from his friends Dr. Johnson, Oliver Goldsmith, Sir Joshua Reynolds, and David Garrick to enable him to withstand the scurrilous attacks made against his design. He did not live to see the completion of his masterpiece ; the south-east corner of the building was not put in hand until the year 1830, when Sir Robert Smirke completed the original design for the river-front and built King's College. The whole of the northern portion of the building fronting the Strand was completed in 1779, ready to house the Royal Academy, and the Royal and other learned societies. Chambers from the outset had considered an extensive frontage to the Strand, of which the finished portion was to form the central feature ; this scheme is one which may yet be realised.

When Sir James Pennethorne carried out the extension of the building fronting Waterloo Bridge he received a well-deserved compliment from seventy-five of his brother professionals in the form of a letter of congratulation.

"LONDON : *July* 1, 1856.

"DEAR SIR,—Your professional brethren are anxious to congratulate you on the successful completion of your design for the western wing of Somerset House, in which at the same time you have adhered to the taste and style of the original edifice and have done full justice to the genius of Chambers, you have adapted these additions to a difficult site with great propriety, and thereby produced a striking architectural feature in the entrance to London by Waterloo Bridge."

Among the signatories to this eulogistic letter were Philip Hardwick, C. R. Cockerell, Charles Barry, Decimus Burton, and Sidney Smirke.

Fergusson's attack on the composition of the façade to the river was not entirely unwarranted, although the alternative design he suggested would not have been any great improvement. Chambers's conception of a series of square terraces rising sheer from the water-line was extremely fine ; like a true artist, he had in mind the unequalled sweep of the river eastwards, and, realising that the silhouette of St. Paul's would form the climax to his picture, he avoided the introduction of elements which would only disturb the sublimity of the scheme as a whole. The great fault of the river-

Plate IV.

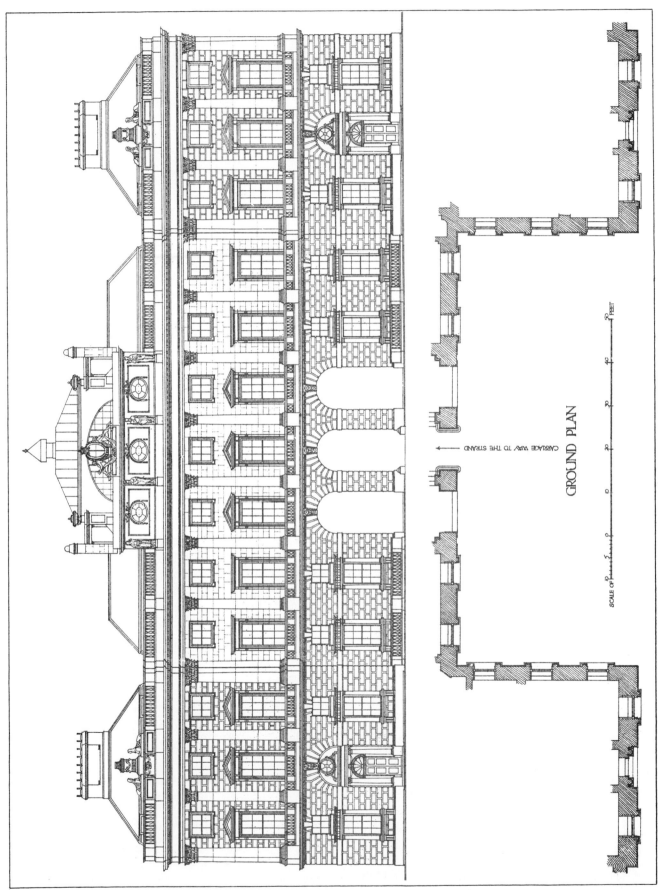

SOMERSET HOUSE, SOUTH FACADE TO COURTYARD.

SIR WILLIAM CHAMBERS, ARCHITECT. 1776.

GROUND PLAN

CARRIAGE WAY TO THE STRAND

SCALE OF FEET

Plate V.

PALLADIAN BRIDGE MOTIF.

OFFICE OF THE REGISTRAR-GENERAL.

SOMERSET HOUSE, LONDON.

SIR WILLIAM CHAMBERS, ARCHITECT.

front is the lack of harmonic proportion between the main vertical masses, as well as the absurdly small scale of the central dome when considered in relation to the extreme length of the structure.

The principles of academic planning followed by Chambers enabled him to achieve a signal success at Somerset House. The great Court of Honour, with its fine central bronze group, when viewed from the vestibule of the Strand entrance, presents an unequalled vista of architectural scenery.

Sir Joshua Reynolds, delivering his ninth discourse on the occasion of the opening of the Royal Academy at its new quarters at Somerset House, in the year 1780, remarked: "This building in which we are now assembled will remain to many future ages an illustrious specimen of the architect's abilities." Like Sir Christopher Wren, Chambers was an eclectic : he brought to bear his sound judgment and good taste on the examples of the past, selecting the gold and discarding the dross preparatory to recasting the

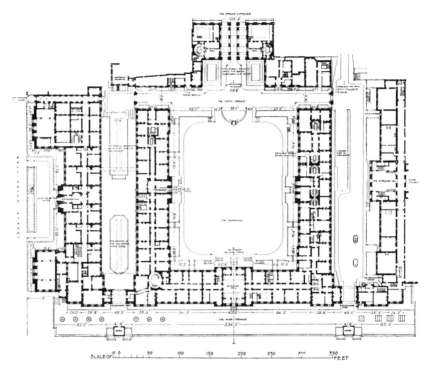

FIG. 18 SOMERSET HOUSE, GENERAL PLAN

metal. Somerset House, unique in position and chaste in design, is a striking example of an academic building worthy of a great nation.

When Chambers first settled in London he purchased a house in Poland Street, where he commenced the practice of his profession. To him came young James Gandon, who was accepted as an indentured pupil at a very moderate fee ; he resided continuously with his master, attending the different schools in the evenings, more particularly that of "Shipley's," until he quitted Chambers's

FIG. 19. SOMERSET HOUSE, STRAND FRONT. DETAIL OF BASEMENT STOREY

FIG. 20. SOMERSET HOUSE, THE VESTIBULE

Sir William Chambers, Architect

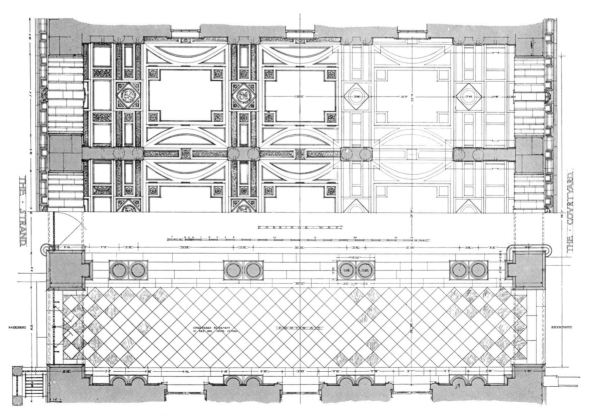

FIG. 21. SOMERSET HOUSE, PLAN OF THE VESTIBULE

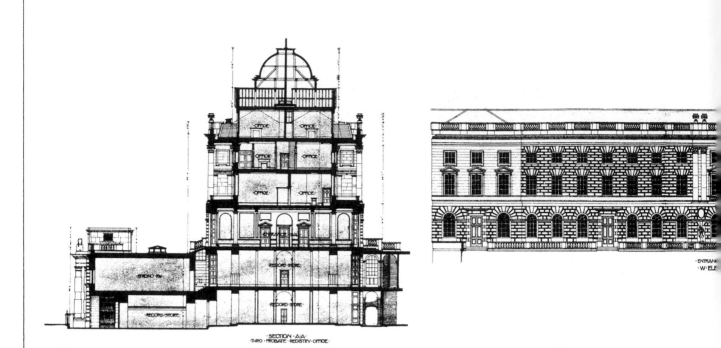

· SECTION · A·A ·
·THRO · PROBATE · REGISTRY · OFFICE ·

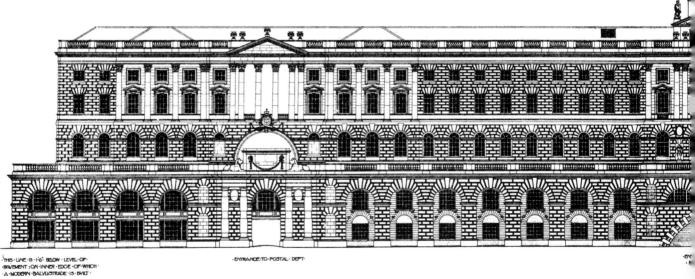

·THIS · LINE · IS · 1'6" · BELOW · LEVEL · OF ·
· PAVEMENT : ON · INNER · EDGE · OF · WHICH ·
· A · MODERN · BALVSTRADE · IS · BVILT ·

· ENTRANCE · TO · POSTAL · DEPT ·

SOMERSET HOUSE, EI
SIR WILLIAM CI
COMPLETED BY SIR ROBERT S

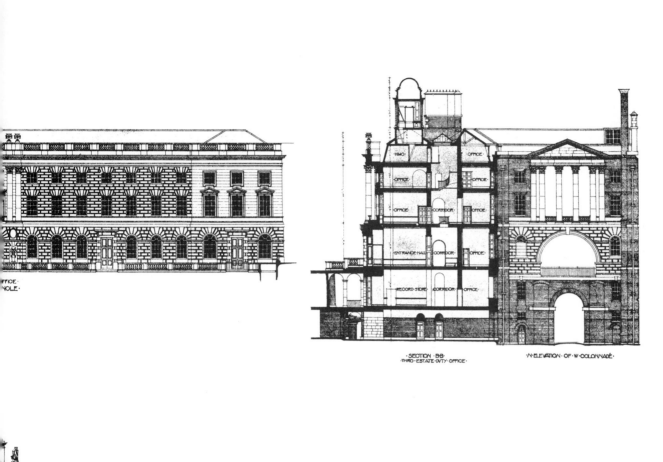

·SECTION ·B·B·
·THRO ·ESTATE ·DVTY· OFFICE·

·N·ELEVATION ·OF ·W ·COLONNADE·

·OFFICE·
·NOLE·

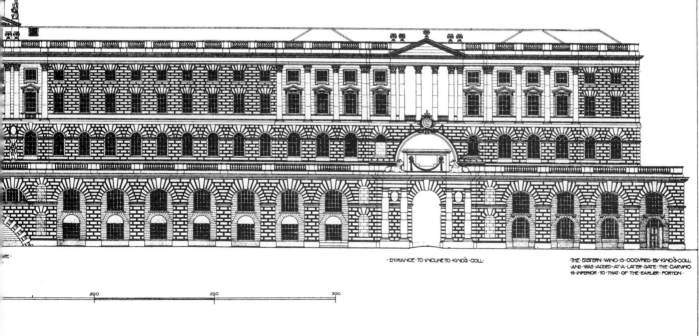

·ENTRANCE ·TO ·INCLINE TO ·KING'S ·COLL·

·THE · EASTERN ·WING ·IS ·OCCUPIED ·BY ·KING'S ·COLL·
·AND ·WAS ·ADDED ·AT ·A ·LATER ·DATE ·THE ·CARVING·
·IS ·INFERIOR ·TO ·THAT ·OF ·THE ·EARLIER ·PORTION·

200   250   300

ON OF RIVER FRONT.

ARCHITECT.

IR JAMES PENNETHORNE.

Plate VIII.

SOMERSET HOUSE, WEST FACADE TO WATERLOO BRIDGE.

SIR JAMES-PENNETHORNE, ARCHITECT, 1852—1856.

Plate IX.

THE CASINO, MARINO CLONTARF. EAST ELEVATION.

THE CASINO, MARINO CLONTARF. SOUTH WEST ELEVATION.

SIR WILLIAM CHAMBERS, ARCHITECT.

Plate X.

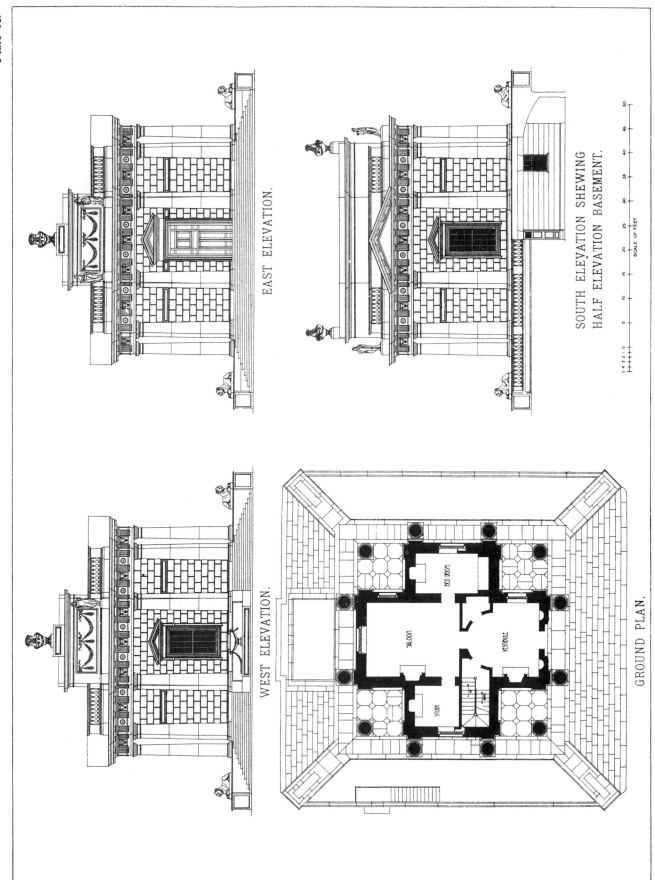

EAST ELEVATION.

SOUTH ELEVATION SHEWING
HALF ELEVATION BASEMENT.

SCALE OF FEET

WEST ELEVATION.

GROUND PLAN.

THE CASINO, MARINO CLONTARF.
SIR WILLIAM CHAMBERS, ARCHITECT.

office. In 1769 the Gold Medal of the Royal Academy was awarded to him for the design of a triumphal arch, and soon after this initial success he commenced the Court House at Nottingham, his first public work. In 1768 Gandon competed with Thomas Cooley and Thomas Sandby for the New Exchange (now the City Hall) in Dublin. His design at the time received much praise, although Cooley's scheme obtained the first premium.

The turning-point in Gandon's career was reached when Lord Carlow wrote in 1779 asking him to take up an appointment in Ireland. This he accepted, and after a great deal of trouble with the Dublin Corporation he commenced building the Customs House in July 1781. The structure, when completed, proved to be his chief work, and incidentally the bed-rock of academic architecture in Ireland. During the progress of this building he undertook the design of the Court House and gaol for Waterford. In 1785 it was decided to carry out alterations to the old Parliament House. Gandon was appointed for the work, and added the Corinthian portico as an entrance to the House of Lords. After the death of Cooley, Gandon undertook the completion of the Four Courts, the west wing of which had alone been completed. Cooley's scheme for the building he considerably improved, but he allowed certain features designed

FIG. 22. SOMERSET HOUSE, DETAIL OF PALLADIAN ARCH MOTIF

by his predecessor to remain. One great improvement was certainly effected when the central mass of the building was brought nearer the river, thereby enabling the whole composition to be viewed in connection with the distant Customs House. The wisdom of this procedure became even more apparent when Sir Robert Smirke erected the Wellington Obelisk in Phœnix Park, completing the vista along the north bank of the Liffey, and demonstrating the inestimable value of sympathetic architecture to the scheme of a city.

Prior to the appearance of Gandon in the architectural lists, the civic aspect of Dublin was poor in quality. The most important building then standing was the Parliament House, the newly erected Royal Exchange, by Thomas Cooley, ranking next in merit. And native talent, with the exception of Thomas Ivory, was not very prominent; his chief building, the Blue Coat Hospital, was built in 1773. In fact it was by no means unusual for clients to take up the usual duties of an architect, superintending the design and erection of their own houses. In the majority of instances builders posed as architects, subletting the various trades to incompetent journeymen. Therefore the fullest praise is due to the efforts of the far-seeing men who induced Gandon to take up active practice in Ireland; and with the erection of the Customs House a new era dawned in building circles. The choice of site for such an official structure was in every way advantageous, it provided a magnificent frontage to the River Liffey, being near the North Wall; and moreover was convenient of axis

FIG. 23. THE CUSTOMS HOUSE, DUBLIN *James Gandon, Architect*

from every part of the city. In addition new docks were required in the immediate vicinity, and these were to be considered as forming part of the works ; all the plain warehouses adjoining the Customs House were erected under the direct supervision of Gandon or his pupil, Baker.

Not only was Gandon familiar with the principles of composition enunciated by his former master, Sir William Chambers, but he shared the latter's preference for Roman form and taste for refinement in the selection of ornament. The river façade of the Customs House, with its vigorous Dorian theme, reveals his predilections in this regard. There is inherent in the appropriate character of the building a strength of purpose and a definition unlike that applying to the design of any other contemporary building. There is a total absence and disregard of trivialites. Not only does the building inherit something of the finest attributes of the whole series which preceded its erection, but the amazing skill of the designer imparted to the structure a unique character. Gandon approached his problems as a sculptor first, and a constructor last ; he strove for the maximum effects of light and shade, and never allowed his taste to succumb to the fashionable effeminacies, such as were advocated in other quarters. In the disposition of the minor elements in every part of the building, each feature is an exquisite study in itself, bearing due relation to the larger parts, and supporting the monumental qualities. The care and study displayed in the above arrangement enhance the general effect in a very powerful way, with the resulting gain in impressiveness on the mind of the beholder.

FIG. 24. THE CUSTOMS HOUSE, DUBLIN. BACK ELEVATION *James Gandon, Architect*

To ensure the building appearing conspicuous from the sea, the architect introduced the dome as a central feature in the composition, and in this inheres the chief fault in the design. There exists a lamentable difference between the scale of the huge Doric order to the portico and the delicate Corinthian order forming the peristyle to the dome. Considered as a piece of spirited architecture the latter is admirable in every particular ; it partakes somewhat of the grace of the twin cupola at Greenwich Hospital,

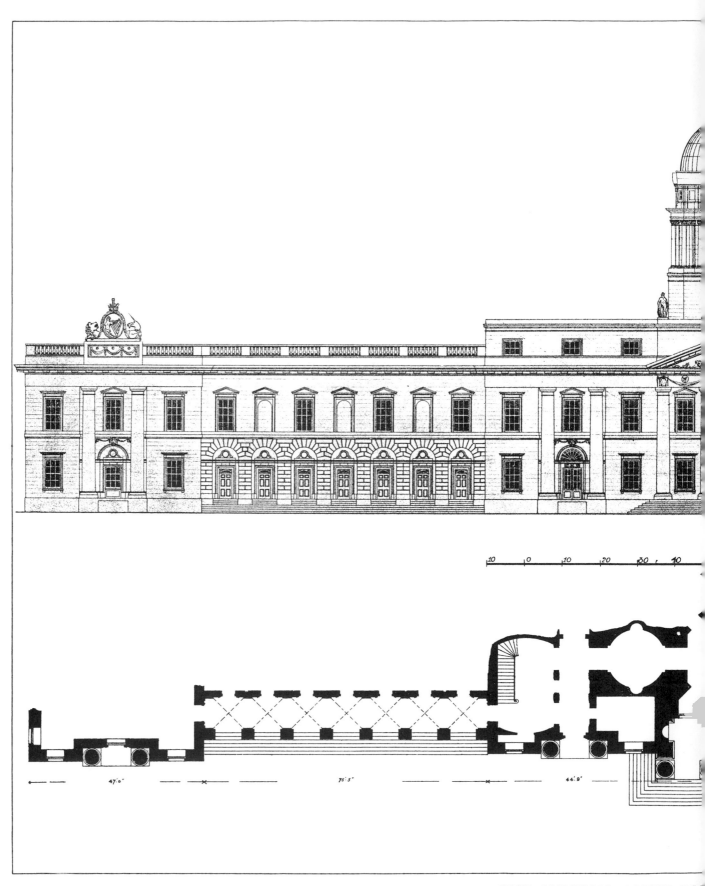

THE CUSTOMS HOUSE, DU

JAMES GANL

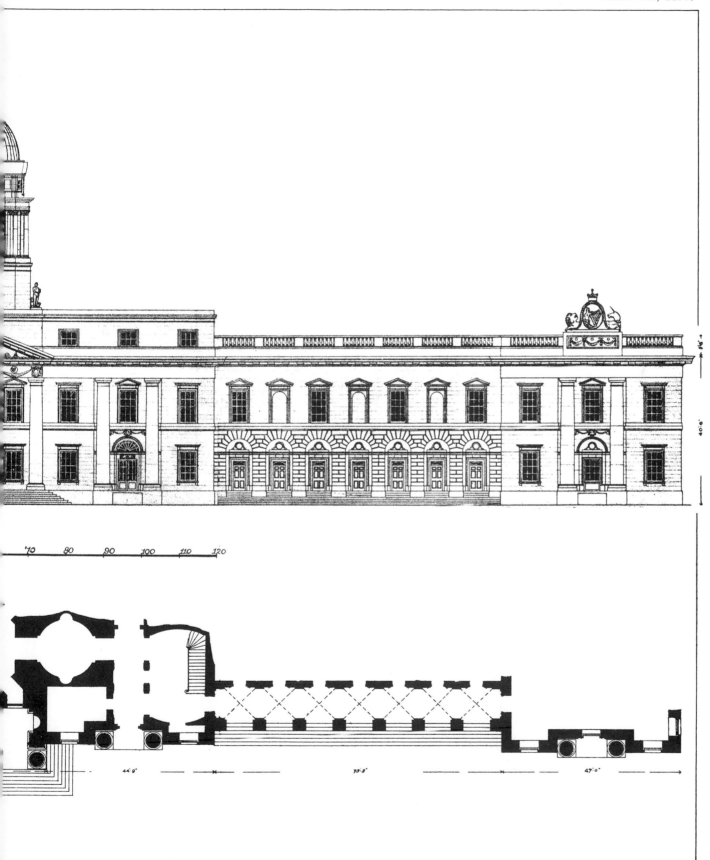

70   80   90   100   110   120

44'9"   73'5"   47'0"

RONT ELEVATION & PLAN.

TECT. 1781.

Plate XIII.

THE CUSTOMS HOUSE, DUBLIN. SOUTH-EAST WING.

JAMES GANDON, ARCHITECT, 1781.

and hints of the greater dome of St. Paul's. The similitude between the situation of Dublin in relation to the Liffey, and London in regard to the Thames, evidently impressed Gandon ; he was thoroughly conversant with the *genius loci* of both places, and as a natural consequence understood the value of a domical feature towering above the horizontal line of a city divided by a river. At the Customs House, although the dome acts as a splendid foil and contrast to the lengthy river façade, the contrast is such as to accentuate the difference in scale between the dome and the portico. While the works were progressing, Gandon obtained models from Carlini, in London, for the sculptured decoration and statuary.

Through the good offices of a Mr. Darley, a young sculptor, Edward Smith was brought to the architect's notice, and after he had prepared models in competition with those submitted by Carlini, he was exclusively employed for the execution of this portion of the work.

In this regard mention must be made of the series of carved keystones, bearing heads of the River gods ; the latter are unsurpassable both as regards design and execution. The four figures, Europe, Asia, Africa, and America, which adorn the north portico are the work of Smith, whilst those above the portico, to the river front, were carried out by Carlini.

The models for the decoration of the interior of the cupola were prepared direct from Gandon's drawings. The richness of the ornament to the interior part of the dome is very striking ; it resembles in relief and quality the elegance of the contemporary French ornament, but it is stronger in modelling, and its interest is maintained by the symbolic character of the constituent elements. His reputation as an exponent of the monumental rests on the world-renowned Customs House, but during his practice in Dublin, he carried out many buildings in the city and its vicinity.

Among these works were the Military Hospital in Phœnix Park (the cupola was added later, and is not Gandon's), Carlisle Bridge, forming the connection between Sackville Street and D'Olier Street, subsequently

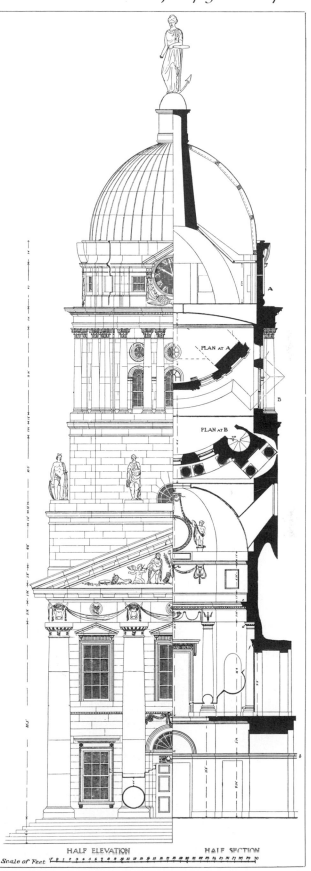

HALF ELEVATION   HALF SECTION

Scale of Feet

FIG. 25. THE CUSTOMS HOUSE, DUBLIN. DETAIL OF PORTICO AND DOME

MONUMENTAL ARCHITECTURE

FIG. 26. THE KING'S INNS, DUBLIN　　　*James Gandon, Architect*

rebuilt and the roadway widened, and the King's Inns or Temple. The last-named is one of the most beautiful buildings in Dublin, and was practically the last work carried into being by Gandon. Its erection occupied nearly five years, 1795–1800, owing to delays and the Rebellion, which forced Gandon to leave Ireland. Neither Sir William Chambers nor his pupil became identified with the furore for Greek art which was occasioned by the publication of Stuart and Revett's book, but the strong following influenced by the teachings of Chambers, could not entirely escape from the widening circle in favour of purity and finesse in detail, which the acceptance of the Greek researches entailed. Nowhere is this truth more clearly apparent than in the works of James Gandon. The coarse ornamentation and the crude detail which disfigured the vigorous creations of the early years of the eighteenth century had given place to studied refinement, gracefulness of outline, and academic charm. In this rich simplicity some prefer to see nothing but coldness; they cannot understand the drastic criticism to which architects submitted their designs; and the desire expressed on all sides to avoid offending the canons of good taste. In Ireland, especially, has this admirable doctrine been observed to the present time, and it is easily attributable to the inspiring tradition engendered by Gandon.

FIG. 27. THE KING'S INNS, DUBLIN. DETAIL OF DOOR-WAY　　　*James Gandon, Architect*

Gandon's connection with the erection of the Court House at Waterford has already been referred to, but a few other facts are of interest. When the idea was first suggested to him, he demurred against undertaking the work, owing mainly to his many engagements in the capital. Eventually his friends persuaded him to prepare the design, and the work was begun in the spring of 1784; and after many delays the building was completed. It is interesting to realise that the majority of Court Houses subsequently erected throughout Ireland have been based on this prototype, and mention must be made of the building at Londonderry, and the exquisite example at Galway.

Gandon's connection with the completion of Thomas Cooley's scheme for the Four Courts dates from the death of the latter in 1784. The building had been started in 1776, and the western wing was completed at a cost of £16,788. But it was entirely owing to Gandon's skill that a great improvement was effected in the composition of the façade and its cohesion with the wings. The dome has

FIG. 28. THE FOUR COURTS, DUBLIN   *Thomas Cooley and James Gandon, Architects*

been subjected to criticism as being devoid of interest, but this defect is more than atoned for by the quiet dignity and correct expression of the structure as a comprehensive whole. In the internal decoration of the rotunda, more especially the domical ceiling, is to be seen the refining hand of Gandon. It is said that the small library at Charlemont House, Dublin, carried out in 1782, is also Gandon's work ; this is more than probable owing to the friendship which existed between Lord Charlemont and the architect, which dated from the time when Sir William Chambers introduced his pupil to the patron.

In 1808, Gandon retired to Lucan, near Dublin, where he resided until his death in 1823, at the advanced age of 82.

His contemporary, Thomas Cooley (1740–84), to some extent anticipated Gandon's practice in Ireland by erecting the Dublin Royal Exchange. His success in this competition induced him to take up his residence in that city, where he designed the Dublin Newgate, the Record Office, the Marine School, and the chapel in the Park, and also prepared the original designs for the Four Courts, which were completed by Gandon.

FIG. 29. THE FOUR COURTS, DUBLIN. THE ROTUNDA
Thomas Cooley and James Gandon, Architects

MONUMENTAL ARCHITECTURE

The design of the Royal Exchange is certainly striking for its refinement and other sterling qualities; the main feature in the planning consisting of the circular rotunda with its unique adjustment to the subsidiary offices. The site offered many advantages, not the least being the fact that it terminated a lengthy vista, hence the introduction of the pedimented portico. There is a delicacy of treatment in Cooley's work, which closely resembles the work of the school of Chambers, but in many respects it is quite distinctive from the contemporary work then proceeding in England, and at first sight appears to be somewhat later in date of erection than is really the case. His design for the prison was hampered by considerations of site and cost, and it was altogether insufficient for its purpose. There can be no shadow of a doubt that had Cooley lived longer he would have proved to be a serious competitor for a share of Gandon's work.

Meanwhile other architects were becoming prominent in England. Among them was George Dance the younger (1740–1825), who, after serving his pupilage in his father's office, then travelled in France and Italy. On his return he competed for the design of Blackfriars Bridge, eventually won by Mylne; in 1768 he succeeded his father in the office of City Architect. Dance was awarded the gold medal of the Academy of Parma in 1763, and in 1764 was elected a member of the Academy of St. Luke at Rome.

In 1770 the City Corporation having decided to proceed with the rebuilding of Newgate, instructed Dance to prepare designs. The problem to be surmounted was the concealment within four walls of a heterogeneous collection of cells and courts in such a manner that the exterior of the building should present an unpierced mass. The resulting composition, based upon a simple Palladian grouping, provided one of the finest monumental structures London has ever seen. It is more than possible that Piranesi's "Carceri d'Invenzione" gave Dance a clue to the character of the various minor features, such as the tooling of the stone wall-surfaces and the use of symbolic *motifs*, but the essential character of the design was English.

Real architecture requires to be molten in the imagination of the designer; to be ready as it were to emerge from such a crucible in one instantaneous gush. Then it attains to such power and significance as to leave an impression, on the mind of all beholders, of a perfect coherent and indivisible whole.

FIG. 30. THE EXCHANGE, NOW THE CITY HALL, DUBLIN   *Thomas Cooley, Architect*

28

Plate XIV.

THE EXCHANGE, NOW THE CITY HALL, DUBLIN. INTERIOR.

THOMAS COOLEY, ARCHITECT. 1770.

Plate XV.

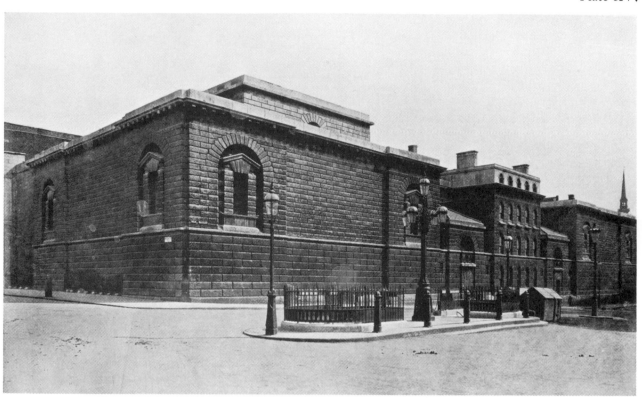

NEWGATE PRISON, LONDON. GENERAL VIEW AND VIEW OF
GOVERNOR'S HOUSE.

GEORGE DANCE, R.A., ARCHITECT, 1770.

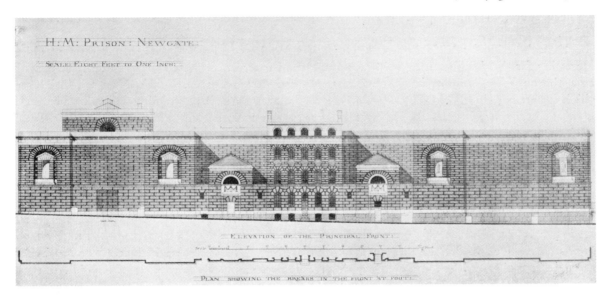

FIG. 31. NEWGATE PRISON, LONDON. ELEVATION OF MAIN FAÇADE   *George Dance, R.A., Architect*

It cannot be said of the majority of the buildings accredited to Dance that they bear sufficient traces of having passed this supreme and exacting simile; Newgate being the exception. In this structure the architect exhibited an imaginative singularity unprecedented in its forcefulness;

forbidding and gloomy in the extreme it certainly is, but far removed from the taint of the merely mechanical. Its gigantic masses, rendered more sombre by the working of the material, symbolised the awful majesty of the place; the rude grandeur of the external aspect hinted mystically of the scenes within.

The prominence given to the Governor's house in the centre of the principal front has been the cause of much criticism, which further analysis of the design may help to clear away. That Dance risked such a contrast in placing a building of domestic character in the midst of a fortress structure, is sufficient proof of his confidence in his own powers; that he succeeded is unquestionable. In the first instance he resolved the composition into three main groups, namely, two balancing wings linked by a recessed centre, in itself a simple grouping. Having obtained a strong contrast in the arrangement of the primary masses, he proceeded to deal with the entrance lodges and the Governor's house, intending the latter as a subordinate grouping to fill the recessed space. By

FIG. 32. NEWGATE PRISON.   DETAIL OF NICHE

George Dance, R.A., Architect

this procedure, in rightly placing a submotif, he fulfilled one of the chief laws of academic design.

Dance's design for All Hallows Church, London Wall, erected in 1765, is a quiet treatment, chiefly interesting for the design of the main wall parallel to the street. The church of St. Alphage, in the same thoroughfare is domestic in character. In the design for St. Luke's Hospital, Old Street, which he erected in 1782, Dance again rose to the occasion and achieved a dignified structure in brick and stone, nearly five hundred feet in length. In 1789 he built the Shakespeare Gallery, in Pall Mall, a building adapted to a narrow site, and which reflected the Græco-Roman manner practised by Holland and the Wyatts.

The Prison or Compter in Giltspur Street, built in 1787, in close proximity to Newgate, echoed the minor characteristics of the latter structure. It was pulled down in 1855.

Dance also effected alterations at the Mansion House, including the removal of the attic storeys. His scheme for the improvement of the Port of London, shown in an engraving by William Daniel, dated 1802, was the last of several designs prepared for a select committee of the House of Commons, engaged in deliberating on the improvements. This scheme included a double bridge, each of six arches, with a drawbridge, and the embankment of the river at this point, near the Tower ; had this scheme been carried into being a congested quarter of the Metropolis would have been cleared. Dance entertained lively recollections of his endeavours in this regard, and when engaged upon the building of Alfred Place and Crescent, between the years 1802–14, he embodied the idea of semicircular ends in this minor scheme. Of greater interest as an example of street architecture is the design for Finsbury Square, built between the years 1777–91. His other public works embrace the theatre at Bath, 1805 ; the Royal College of Surgeons, Lincoln's Inn Fields, in connection with James Lewis ; the south front of the Guildhall, with its curious blend of Gothic and Classic, and the elegant Council Chamber in the same building. His lesser works include country mansions in various parts of England, as well as alterations and additions to such buildings as Lansdowne House, Bowood, etc., etc. Dance's individual manner materially assisted his pupil John Soane to form his opinions, and although Soane's work is in no wise imitative, it nevertheless reveals evidence of Dance's direction.

The last quarter of the eighteenth century was productive of a corresponding change in architectural taste. The Roman Palladian phase imperceptibly blended with the newer information respecting the antique, and there followed important changes, not only in England, but in other countries. This fusion of the vernacular style with purer detail and ornament contributed in a great measure to the Græco-Roman phase which marks the next stage in the development.

ORNAMENT FROM THE PALLADIAN LOGGIA, SOMERSET HOUSE

CHAPTER III

THE GRÆCO-ROMAN PHASE, 1780–1820

STUART AND REVETT—HENRY HOLLAND—THOMAS HARDWICK—S. P. COCKERELL—THOMAS HARRISON—JAMES WYATT—JEFFREY WYATT—SIR JOHN SOANE—JOHN NASH—GEORGE REPTON—J. JOHNSON—DAVID LAING —THE BROTHERS PAIN—ROBERT REID—CHARLES HEATHCOTE TATHAM— GEORGE LEDWALL TAYLOR—JOHN LINNELL BOND—THE RENNIES (FATHER AND SON)—WILLIAM TIERNEY CLARK

THE accession of George III. to the throne of England in the year 1760 is the most conspicuous landmark in the history of the eighteenth century. It concurred with a new *régime* of progress, consolidation, and reform, appertaining not only to the sphere of politics and commerce, but also to the realm of education, science, and art.

During the eventful period which ensued England suffered humiliation by the revolt and separation of the American colonies, she withstood the turmoil of the French Revolution, and wrestled intermittently with her mighty enemy, Napoleon, for the hegemony of the world. Through the agency of her commercial enterprises, and more particularly the East India Company, she established the nucleus of her overseas empire. As a result the merchant princes became powers in the State and began to encroach on the social privileges of the old courtly aristocracy, as well as to engage with equal zest in the pursuit of knowledge and artistic culture.

The foundation of the Royal Academy in the year 1768 further advanced the development of the fine arts. The artist and the architect were elevated to a higher plane in the public estimation, and the standard of taste, regulated by the critical tribunal, became formal and refined. Among the leaders of artistic thought were Reynolds, Gainsborough, and Chambers ; while Garrick, Kean, and Mrs. Siddons enthralled the public with their dramatic genius, and Dr. Johnson raised the standard of English literature. The increased growth of the residential centres beyond the confines of the City foreshadowed the town-planning schemes of the Regency epoch ; the great manufacturing cities of the Midlands and North Country sprang up from a collection of obscure towns. Steam power was invented and machinery called into being, science and research were fostered by the Royal Society and the Society of Antiquaries ; an architectural era began remarkable for the erection of a vast number of public buildings and engineering works. The great church-building period identified with the life of Sir Christopher Wren had given place to a period of private palace building, which in turn was displaced by a more important period, during which the erection of public and official structures proceeded apace. This latter period reflected the stirring events of the sixty years' reign of George III., while the Continent rocked in the throes of revolution and war. It is not, however, with the early part of this illustrious reign that the Græco-Roman phase of English Neo-Classic is connected, although the events which occasioned the subtle change in style had their birth practically at its beginning. In the main the extension of archæological research by Englishmen to the shores of Greece was the responsible factor, when in the year 1751 Stuart and Revett started their explorations at Athens, the results of which were published in 1762. How this far-reaching movement was caused is best explained by quoting the words of the preface of the " Ionian Antiquities " (1796), that

" In the year 1734 some gentlemen who had travelled in Italy, desirous of encouraging at home a taste for those objects which had contributed so much to their entertainment abroad, formed themselves into a society under the name of the Dilettanti, and agreed upon such resolutions as they thought necessary to keep up the spirit of the scheme."

The formation of the society encouraged architects and artists, and latterly amateurs, to extend

31

their studies to Greece in search of precise information concerning the architecture of the older civilisation. This resulted in the series of authoritative volumes starting with Stuart and Revett's "Antiquities of Athens," and continuing with the scientific works of Cockerell and Penrose, which have since served as models for all subsequent publications treating of Classic art. The early date of the movement is all the more remarkable considering the difficulties attached to travelling in those days. The Turkish domination of the Levant had yet to be broken by the battle of Navarino ; the isles of the Archipelago teemed with pirates, and on the mainland the superstition of the natives had to be overcome before access could be gained to the ruins. Even the French, contrary to their customary enterprise in matters of archæology, neglected Greece and confined their researches to Rome. Therefore to England belongs the honour of directing Europe to the purer sources of antique architecture.

The labours of the English archæologists, exact and convincing as disclosed by their published works, found ready acceptance on the Continent. In Germany they inspired the writings of Winckelmann, and gave Langhans the suggestion to impart a monumental Greek character to the Brandenburger Thor at Berlin. In France the new information, although anticipated by Le Roy's book, was eagerly received, although not so readily adapted to the prevailing tradition, but in the subsequent hardening of the style Louis Seize is discernible the germ of the Greek character so characteristic of the style of the Empire, evolved thirty years later by Percier and Fontaine.

James Stuart returned to England a renowned architect, and became an arbiter of taste in fashionable circles, although he did not receive a great number of commissions. His first building, Lord Anson's house, No. 15 St. James's Square, was one in which he showed the adaptability of Greek detail to the vernacular style. This design demonstrated how the spirit of Hellenic art could be interpreted without having recourse to mere reproduction, an important achievement which many of Stuart's successors failed to accomplish. He realised the limitations imposed on architectural design if the latter policy was resorted to, and skilfully avoided this fault by building in accordance with the Roman Palladian style of the day, merely applying his knowledge of Greek finesse to the columns, entablatures, and minor elements. His other works included alterations to Spencer House, overlooking St. James's Park, which had been previously built by Vardy ; Attingham Hall, Shropshire ; and the infirmary and the beautiful chapel at Greenwich Hospital (illustrated in "Later Renaissance Architecture in England," Messrs. Belcher and Macartney's important book).

At Shugborough, Staffordshire, the seat of Lord Anson, he carried into execution several works, employing as motifs, the arch of Hadrian, the octagonal Tower of the Winds, and the choragic monument of Lysicrates. In 1760, at a period when Portman Square was building, he designed the house with the projecting portico for Mrs. Montague, and later built his own house, No. 45 Harley Street.

Among the many famous architects whose works adorned the second half of the

FIG. 33. No. 15 ST. JAMES'S SQUARE, S.W. *James Stuart, Architect*

eighteenth century, including such masters as Chambers and Gandon themselves, there is not one whose influence was destined to be felt so strongly, at a later period, than that of this shrewd Scotsman. Chambers fought shy of the newer teaching, and Gandon, while professing great curiosity as to why Greek architecture should be so much extolled, continued with his opinions concerning that of Rome.

Stuart, however, was an energetic, persistent man who had achieved fame in the sphere of archæology long before he essayed the more difficult task of design. His drawings and writings were distinguished alike for the accuracy of the information, as well as for the enterprise they evinced. Stuart himself practised the doctrines he advocated, but the opportunities which occurred for him to demonstrate his talent were few; and in consequence others reaped the benefit. Yet his pioneer labours instantly acted as a check to the prevalent style, and while they aided the volition of the Adam's manner on the one hand; by reason of their sequence and iron restraint, on the other hand, they imposed the cult of the academic on all having recourse to the principles expounded. It might be argued that the very simplicity of Stuart's designs to some extent militate against their being considered as inspiring; formal they certainly are,

FIG. 34. GREENWICH HOSPITAL CHAPEL. MARBLE ORGAN LOFT
James Stuart, Architect

but of that formality which is the very life of refinement; and while standing out in clear definition amidst other works of this period, although intimately related to the latter, they, notwithstanding, bear an air of unrivalled distinction.

Stuart's partner in his Athenian explorations, Nicholas Revett, does not appear to have had an extensive practice. For Sir Lionel Lyde he built the chapel at Ayot St. Lawrence, in Hertfordshire, a building inspired in detail by the Dorian temples of Sicily, although the general composition was in the vernacular style. His other works were limited to the eastern and western porticoes of Lord Spencer's house at West Wycombe and some temples in the grounds; at Standlynch, in Wiltshire, he added a portico to the eastern front for Mr. Dawkins.

But Revett's energies were mainly centred on archæological research, which pursuit he faithfully developed with Stuart, although the time came when he quarrelled with his quondam colleague over

MONUMENTAL ARCHITECTURE

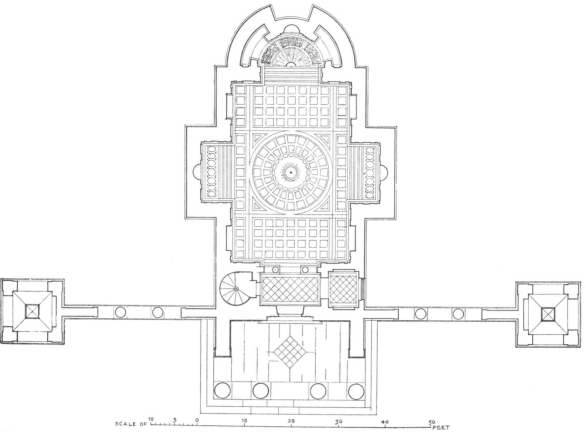

SCALE OF 10 5 0 10 20 30 40 50 FEET

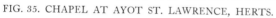

FIG. 35. CHAPEL AT AYOT ST. LAWRENCE, HERTS.

Nicholas Revett, Architect

FIG. 36. CHAPEL AT AYOT ST. LAWRENCE, HERTS. THE INTERIOR

Nicholas Revett, Architect

34

the publication of certain drawings intended for the "Antiquities." Meanwhile, architectural events were proceeding apace, the finesse of Greek detail had percolated down to the various trades, and apart from the coterie of craftsmen who supplied chimney-pieces, fitments, furniture, and other accessories, to the order of the brothers Adam, every journeyman carpenter was also conversant with the refinement and beauty of Greek architecture, as set forth by the publication of the scientific

volumes. As a consequence there resulted an immediate improvement in the character of the minor features mentioned above. Shop-fronts and door casings were also among the features which first reflected the change in taste; and in this regard deserve consideration, although their subject is outside the limits of this work. Yet, regarded as a whole, the movement which characterised the second half of the eighteenth century was wonderfully consistent, and this in spite of the diversity of opinion as to the correct interpretation of the "Classic Spirit." If an illustration were required

FIG. 37. DOVER HOUSE, WHITEHALL, 1786   *Henry Holland, Architect*

to show how the early phases of the movement overlapped it will be found in the career of Henry Holland (1744–1806). He was in practice contemporaneously with Sir Robert Taylor, Sir William Chambers, and the brothers Adam, nevertheless he managed to attract attention as the originator of the Græco-Roman style. In the year 1777–78 he designed and erected Brooks's Club-house, No. 60 St. James's Street, the front of which has since been partially altered. About 1780 he followed the example of the brothers Adam, and, entering upon the field of speculative finance, he purchased about forty acres of land in Chelsea, laid out Sloane Street, Cadogan Place, and Hans Place, and erected the houses on the west side of Sloane Street. In 1786 he designed for the Duke of York the charming Greek Ionic portico and the circular-domed vestibule to Featherstonehaugh

House, Whitehall (afterwards Melbourne and Dover House), and this was his first essay in monumental architecture. In 1788 followed work of importance at Carlton House, Pall Mall, for the Prince of Wales, afterwards George IV. Holland made considerable alterations to the earlier building, which had been designed by Hilcroft in 1733, forming a magnificent suite of rooms, and extending the north façade to 195 feet in length. The order employed for the main front was Roman Corinthian, and embraced two storeys. The portico in the centre was designed as a gigantic

FIG. 38. CARLTON HOUSE, PALL MALL, 1788.   VIEW SHOWING SCREEN
Henry Holland, Architect

porte cochère, and in this regard was one of the first of its kind to be erected in England. The whole building was partially screened from the public gaze by means of an elegant colonnade. When Carlton House was demolished in 1827, on account of the "Metropolitan improvements," the columns and some of the capitals were stored to be used at a later date by William Wilkins for the façade of the National Gallery. Holland enjoyed considerable fame during the closing years of the eighteenth century as a theatre architect. At that time there were no other serious competitors for this class of work. The brothers Adam had prepared a grandiose scheme for a National Opera House in the Haymarket, but this never came to maturity, and when they died Holland had a clear field. In 1791 he designed Drury Lane Theatre for R. B. Sheridan, built at a cost of about £200,000. This structure was opened in March 1797, but was destroyed by fire on February 24, 1809. Covent Garden Theatre was remodelled by him in 1794, and was also burnt to the ground in 1808. In 1799 Holland was in competition against Dance and Soane for the design of the East India Company's new building, 190 feet in length. This building has been erroneously attributed to R. Jupp, presumably because he was surveyor to the company. The façade exhibited the usual pedimented portico and Greek Ionic order affected by Holland ; in composition it was not entirely successful, owing to the appendages being badly connected to the central feature. This façade was some time after taken as a model by Francis Johnston for the front of the Post Office in Sackville Street, Dublin. In 1804 the remodelling of the Albany in Piccadilly was entrusted to Holland, a work which embodied the conversion of the mansion designed by Sir William Chambers into suites of bachelor apartments, with extensive additions at the back. The houses on either side of the entrance lodge in Vigo Street were erected by him at the same time. His last monumental design of importance, completed in 1807, was the colonnaded screen wings and pavilions to the Glasgow Assembly Rooms, previously built by the brothers Adam. In 1799 he succeeded R. Jupp as surveyor to the East India Company, in turn being succeeded by S. P. Cockerell in 1806. Among his pupils were John Soane, Henry Rowles, his nephew, and J. Crunden. His style can be summarised as having been derived from the Palladian vernacular of the time, leavened with Græco-Roman detail. Holland's interior decorations resemble Louis Seize *motifs*, and in this respect they are more robust than those designed by the brothers Adam, as well as being similar in character to many of the interior designs by Chambers.

As the knowledge of the antique became more widely known, so the Græco-Roman phase was developed on more academic lines. Many architects had perforce to obtain their information from illustrated volumes dealing with the subject, but the majority continued to travel abroad, if not to Greece, at least to Rome. Among other young architects who at this time were about to start on their foreign travels were Thomas Hardwick, Thomas Harrison, and John Soane.

Thomas Hardwick was born in 1752. He became the pupil of Sir William Chambers, and in 1769 obtained the first Royal Academy Silver Medal in the class of architecture. In 1777 he travelled on the Continent, spending some considerable time in Rome, where he made measured drawings of the Colosseum and the Pantheon. A model of the former building made from his drawings is in the British Museum, while his measured drawings of the Pantheon are preserved in the library of the Royal Institute of British Architects. His most noted executed building is the large parish church of St. Mary-le-bone, built in 1813–17, at a cost of £30,000. Turner, the landscape-painter, was for a time in Hardwick's office, where he endeavoured to study architecture as a profession ; eventually he took Hardwick's advice and followed the sister art. The many classic architectural groupings which occur in the more important of Turner's pictorial compositions were the outcome of his experience in an architect's office. Hardwick instructed several pupils who afterwards became famous ; among these were his son, Philip Hardwick, Samuel Angell, and John Foulston, who gained reputation as the West of England "Classicist."

One of the most important architects who practised during the later years of the eighteenth century and the early part of the nineteenth was S. P. Cockerell (1754–1827). He was a pupil of Sir Robert Taylor contemporarily with John Nash ; and in after-life he held the position of surveyor to the Sees of Canterbury and London, the Foundling Hospital, the Pulteney and other estates, also to the East India Company and the Board of Admiralty. His classic works comprise the fine western tower to the Church of St. Anne, Soho, the official residence for the First Lord of the Admiralty, the Bishop of London's house, 32 St. James's Square (the details were designed by his son C. R. Cockerell), and a monumental tower to Lord Nelson at Middleton Hall, erected in 1795. His pupils were Joseph Kay, Benjamin Latrobe (who emigrated to America and built the Capitol at Washington, U.S.A.), W. Porden, C. H. Tatham (the author of the "Etchings of Greek and Roman Detail"), and his son C. R. Cockerell.

No architect of the period did more by his personal efforts to advance Classic taste than Thomas Harrison. He was born in 1744, of humble origin, and owing to his eventually being brought to the notice of Lord Dundas he was sent, at that nobleman's expense, to Italy with Cuitt, the landscape-painter. In 1770, while at Rome, he made a design for the decoration of the cortile of the Vatican Belvedere, which, although it obtained the approval of Pope Clement XIV., was not carried out. He became a member of the

FIG. 39. THE CASTLE, CHESTER, 1793–1820   *Thomas Harrison, Architect*

Academy of St. Luke, with a seat on the council of that body, after he had prepared plans for the alteration and embellishment of the Piazza del Popolo; Piranesi drew up an elaborate statement of the circumstances connected with the adjudication of this plan. He returned to London in 1776, and designed the bridge over the river Lune, Lancashire, in 1783, the whole structure being completed in 1788. This bridge was the first level bridge erected in England, and anticipated John Rennie's structure at Kelso.

His great opportunity as a monumental architect came when his plans were selected in competition for rebuilding the Castle at Chester. The works projected for the scheme included a prison, county courts, armoury, exchequer, and gateway, the erection of which extended over many years, 1793–1820. Harrison for this design adopted a version of Greek Doric, which he cleverly arranged to suit the conditions of the problem.

In 1796 he designed Broom Hall, Fifeshire, and when the Earl of Elgin was appointed Ambassador to the Porte in 1799 it was Harrison who suggested to him the importance to England of a collection of drawings and casts of the works of art at Athens and other places in Greece. The noble Earl took the advice of his architect, and made the collection purchased by the Government in 1816 for £35,000, and now known as the Elgin Marbles.

Harrison made a design for a triumphal bridge over the Thames, where Waterloo Bridge now stands, and at a later date was instrumental in causing the company who projected that scheme to employ John Rennie to execute the present structure.

At Liverpool he designed the Athenæum and the Lyceum and the library of the Literary Society, 1799; the tower of the Church of St. Nicholas, 1810–11; the News Room at Chester and the North Gate, 1808, using the Greek Doric order; at Manchester the theatre burnt in 1843 and the Athenæum, also the Exchange (1806–08). In 1810 he erected the monumental group of obelisks on Moel Vamman, N. Wales, to commemorate the fiftieth year of the reign of George III. The triumphal arch on Holyhead Harbour was also designed by him to commemorate the landing of George IV.

In 1821 the celebrated Grosvenor Bridge over the Dee at Chester was carried out by Jesse Hartley, C.E., of Liverpool, who adhered to Harrison's design. Harrison also appears to have been consulted by the then Russian Ambassador to England, Count Woronzow, and about 1822 designed a palace

FIG. 40. INTERIOR OF THE PANTHEON, OXFORD STREET, 1770 *James Wyatt, Architect*

which was built in the Ukraine, Kief, on the river Dneiper. Among his pupils was John Hargreave, of Cork, who carried out extensive Classic works in Ireland.

The late eighteenth century produced no greater exponent of academic architecture than James Wyatt (1746–1813), who was also the most prominent architect of that renowned family of architects the Wyatts. When only fourteen years old he attracted the attention of Lord Bagot, who took him to Rome in order that he might study architecture. After three or four years spent at the capital he travelled to Venice and studied for two years under Visentini. In 1766 he returned to England, designing in 1770 the Pantheon, Oxford Street (the front only now exists), at a cost of £60,000 ; the entrance from Poland Street was built in 1800. In 1796, when the death of Sir William Chambers occasioned a vacancy, Wyatt was appointed Surveyor-General to the Board of Works. In 1770 he was elected Associate of the Royal Academy, in 1785 an Academician, and in 1813 he became President-Elect. The Pantheon in Oxford Street soon after its completion became the fashionable meeting-place for the aristocracy of the day. Wyatt in consequence came into prominence as a society architect, and from that time his success was assured. Trinity House, Tower Hill (1793–97), was built by his brother Samuel Wyatt, but James claimed the design. In 1779 he designed No. 9 Conduit Street, now the Royal Institute of British Architects, and in the same year the houses on the south side of Grosvenor Square. His masterpiece was the interior of the Pantheon, destroyed by fire in 1792, the building being subsequently converted into a theatre. Wyatt's Roman studies gave him the theme for this structure, which consisted of an adaptation of antique prototypes, namely, the Pantheon for its dome—hence the name of the structure—and a super-imposed treatment of the Ionic and Corinthian orders.

Wyatt worked in a more robust manner than the brothers Adam : in this respect his work resembles Holland's. Between the years 1771–1813 he was entrusted with the design and repair of a large number of country mansions, as well as with many restorations of Gothic cathedrals.

His brothers, Samuel Wyatt (1737–1807) (who was architect for Trinity House) and Joseph Wyatt (1739–1818), were both practising architects. Benjamin Dean Wyatt (1775–1850) was the eldest son of James Wyatt, and became his pupil and assistant, afterwards travelling on the

Plate XVI.

THE BANK OF ENGLAND, LONDON. THE COURT ROOM.

SIR ROBERT TAYLOR, ARCHITECT, 1756.

Plate XVII.

THE BANK OF ENGLAND, LONDON. LOTHBURY ANGLE.
SIR JOHN SOANE, ARCHITECT. 1788-1835.

THE GRÆCO-ROMAN PHASE, 1780—1820

Continent in pursuit of his architectural studies. In 1811 he commenced the rebuilding of Drury Lane Theatre, and completed Sir R. Smirke's building, York House, St. James's, from the ground level. In 1828 he built Apsley House for the Duke of Wellington, and in the same year designed with his brother Philip the Oriental Club in Hanover Square. Between the years 1831–34 he carried out the Doric column erected in memory of the Duke of York in Carlton Gardens, at a cost of £25,000. The latter structure forms a splendid composition with the terraces designed by John Nash and his nephew Pennethorne.

Jeffrey Wyatt (1766–1840) was a nephew of James Wyatt. After 1829, on the occasion of receiving a knighthood from George IV., he changed his name to Wyatville. His principal Classic works were a monumental tower in Lincolnshire, 1811, a column in the park at Ashridge, for the Earl of Bridgewater, a Temple of the Graces at Woburn, and the sculpture gallery and various alterations to Holland's

FIG. 41. THE PANTHEON, OXFORD STREET. EXTERIOR VIEW FROM AN OLD PRINT   *James Wyatt, Architect*

work there, 1818–20. At Chatsworth he added the north wing and tower, as well as the Sheffield and Derby entrances, between the years 1821–32. His most important work was the remodelling of Windsor Castle, for which he received the knighthood before mentioned.

In the decoration of the interior apartments, the architect had recourse to an anglicised version of the Empire style, treated in a broad but not particularly delicate manner ; but the correct and main stimulus in this connection was imparted by the taste of Thomas Hope and John Papworth.

The career of Sir John Soane (1753–1837) was of supreme importance to the development of the academic style, because his life's work forms the main connection between two important phases. At the age of fifteen he entered the office of George Dance, and continued with him during the preparation of drawings for the rebuilding of Newgate, afterwards working in Holland's office until 1776.

Sir William Chambers was much impressed by young Soane's abilities, and on the occasion of his winning the Royal Academy Gold Medal in 1776 introduced him to

FIG. 42. TRINITY HOUSE, TOWER HILL, LONDON, 1793–97
          Samuel Wyatt, Architect

King George III., who nominated him Travelling Student. He regarded this event as the most important in his life, and in his " Memoirs" records : " It was the means by which I formed these connections to which I owe all the advantages I have since enjoyed."

MONUMENTAL ARCHITECTURE

While in Italy Soane worked indefatigably in the same field where formerly had laboured Michael Angelo, Vignola, Peruzzi, and Palladio ; he also visited Pæstum and Naples in his quest for fresh inspiration, and intended extending his travels to Athens, but this idea was not realised. In 1780 he returned to England to commence a widespread practice. His patron, Lord Camelford, by his influence secured for Soane the appointment of architect to the Bank of England in 1788, an office which he held until his resignation in 1835. In 1806 he was appointed Professor of Architecture at the Royal Academy, and finally became one of the members of the " Committee of Taste," when the Metropolitan improvements of the " Regency " were under consideration. Many adverse opinions have been expressed concerning Sir John Soane's work ; even during his life it was subject to drastic criticism ; an attack on his facetiously termed " Bœotian " style appeared in Knight's *Quarterly Magazine* in 1824, of which his own son was supposed to be the author. The Bank of England must be regarded as his masterpiece. In 1736 George Sampson erected the nucleus of the present structure near the Church of St. Christopher, and on the site of what is now the centre of the Threadneedle Street front ; Sampson's rear façade still exists, being preserved by Soane during the remodelling. Between the years 1766–86 Sir Robert Taylor added two wings, which he modelled on the design of the Belvedere at the Vatican. In massing Taylor's composition was very effective, and so impressed Soane that he embodied the same idea in the further remodelling which he undertook later. The plan of the Bank epitomises the procedure of rebuilding. A clearance of the site was not permitted ; the old building had to be incorporated with the new, and this process extended over forty-five years. The exterior design of the Bank has hitherto been erroneously regarded as a work designed and completed within a short time. In the first place the architect was considerably handicapped by the retention of Sampson's building, which,

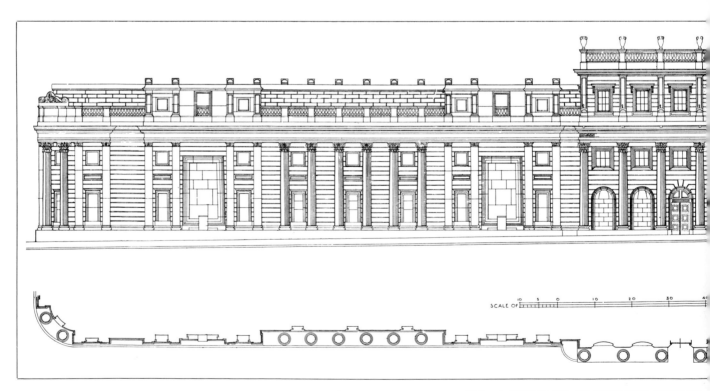

FIG. 43. THE BANK OF ENGLAND, LONDON

THE GRÆCO-ROMAN PHASE, 1780—1820

together with the difference in the levels of the four surrounding roads, made the adoption of an imposing entrance impossible from the outset. In the second place the rebuilding was contemplated piecemeal, a factor of serious importance when the combination of old buildings with new is attempted. Soane's knowledge of academic planning enabled him to meet the peculiar circumstances of the problem ; and if reference is made to the plan his difficulties will be seen. Later on the screen wall was carried completely round to meet the internal arrangements, and in this particular the design resembles the method employed by George Dance in his design for Newgate.

Sir John Soane was the most original architect of the eighteenth century. An extremely able Classicist, he imparted to his works a rare elegance and finish, the result of care, taste, and continual study. From Piranesi's etchings he profited much, as portions of the interior of the Bank and the Picture Gallery at Dulwich reveal. Strange as it may seem, his earlier works were his best. The entrance gateway from the Lothbury courtyard at the Bank is an admirable instance of his monumental work ; next in merit ranks the circular end joining the Princes Street and Lothbury façades. Most of his critics objected to his partiality for tattooing buildings by means of grooves and key patterns ; this practice he undoubtedly carried to an extreme. Seldom content with a first impression when making a design, he prepared innumerable alternatives ; his work in a measure shows this lack of decision. When Professor Cockerell altered the Bank in 1850 he found it necessary to mask the roof of the new Private Drawing Office. This necessitated the improvement of the Threadneedle Street façade, which the Professor accomplished by clearing away Soane's meretricious ornaments, and substituting in their stead a dignified attic. Sir John Soane in his later years aimed at an original style, and this was his weakness ; while he kept to the spirit of the academic Classic he achieved a great deal, but when he attempted to be daringly original he fell into the same pitfall that awaits

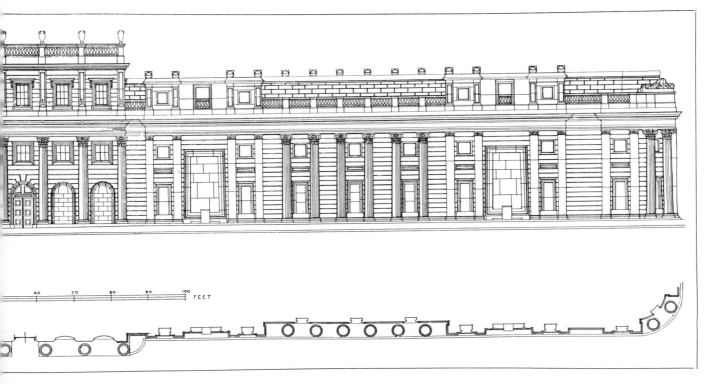

FAÇADE TO THREADNEEDLE STREET

MONUMENTAL ARCHITECTURE

all who have like desires. It is surprising that a man with Sir John Soane's reputation should not have had a great number of imitators, instead of the few who flattered him. During his professorship at the Royal Academy he delivered some remarkably good lectures which approached the story of architecture from the standpoint of design and adaptation, a course which might well be followed at the present day. These lectures created a lasting impression on the minds of all who were privileged to hear them, and their ultimate effect was felt throughout the nineteenth century.

Soane was one of the first English architects to seriously undertake rendering a building fireproof, as well as one of the first to attempt the realisation of a central system of heating, both of which he accomplished with success at the Bank. He understood the inestimable value to an architect of a good library and collection of architectural data, and for his lectures at the Academy he prepared a vast number of diagrams, as well as accurate models of ancient buildings made in Paris by Fouquet. In 1833 he obtained an Act of Parliament settling his museum and collection for the use of the public in perpetuity. Among his most important buildings were Buckingham House, Pall Mall, 1790–94, distinguished for the staircase; the banking house in Fleet Street for Messrs. Praeds and Co., 1801; and New Bank Buildings in Princes Street, Lothbury, 1808–10.* The latter were particularly mentioned by the late Professor Aitchison in his lecture on excellence in architecture. In 1812 he designed and erected the the Dulwich Picture Gallery and Mausoleum, a refined but somewhat exotic composition. Next followed a group of premises in Regent Street, Nos. 156–172, built between the years

FIG. 44. THE BANK OF ENGLAND, LONDON. GROUND PLAN

1820–21. His work at the Westminster Law Courts continued from 1820 to 1827, and during this period he was engaged in building the Scala Regia and the Royal Library in the House of Lords. Trinity Church, Marylebone, was erected between the years 1824–28. The Board of Trade offices in Whitehall, built between the years 1824–27, was previous to the alterations carried out by Sir Charles Barry, a well-considered design, but Soane's original conception was never realised in its entirety. His design for the State-Paper Office, completed in 1833, showed a leaning towards the Italian treatment, and this building is practically the last he personally designed. Among the more renowned of his pupils were David Laing, Sir Robert Smirke, John Sanders, G. Basevi, H. Parke, D. Mocatta, J. Gandy, and C. J. Richardson.

The professional career of John Nash (1752–1835) is so closely connected with the "Metropolitan improvements of the ' Regency ' period " that it must be considered as the prime agency then at work for the betterment of London. Nash was a pupil of Sir Robert Taylor, contemporarily with S. P. Cockerell and others. After some years spent in London he became independent and retired to Carmarthen. His friend S. P. Cockerell, while on a visit to him, fired his dormant enthusiasm for architecture, and in consequence he again took up practice. He proved to be a man of daring enterprise and great capacity for town-planning conceptions; his work in this connection included the opening up of the West End and the creation of a new residential district at Regent's Park.

* These were pulled down in 1896.

Plate XVIII.

THE BANK OF ENGLAND, LONDON. ENTRANCE FROM LOTHBURY COURTYARD.
SIR JOHN SOANE, ARCHITECT. 1788-1835.

Plate XIX.

THREADNEEDLE STREET ANGLE.

VIEW IN GOVERNOR'S COURTYARD.

THE BANK OF ENGLAND, LONDON.

SIR JOHN SOANE, ARCHITECT, 1788–1835.

Plate XX.

THE PRIVATE DRAWING OFFICE.

THE BANK OF ENGLAND, LONDON.

SIR JOHN SOANE, ARCHITECT 1788-1835.

THE PUBLIC DRAWING OFFICE.

PROFESSOR C. R. COCKERELL, R.A. ARCHITECT 1848.

Plate XXI.

PUBLIC CORRIDOR, FORMING NORTH SIDE
OF GOVERNOR'S COURTYARD.

THE BANK OF ENGLAND, LONDON.

SIR JOHN SOANE, ARCHITECT.

ELEVATION OF NORTH FAÇADE IN GOVERNOR'S
COURTYARD.

Plate XXII.

LOGGIA IN LOTHBURY COURTYARD.

CENTRE OF THREADNEEDLE STREET FAÇADE, MASKING SAMPSON'S BUILDING.
THE BANK OF ENGLAND, LONDON.

SIR JOHN SOANE, ARCHITECT.

Plate XXIII.

ENTRANCE VESTIBULE, FROM PRINCES STREET.   TREASURY CORRIDOR.

THE BANK OF ENGLAND, LONDON.

SIR JOHN SOANE, ARCHITECT.

Plate XXIV.

PUBLIC DRAWING OFFICE.

CONSOLS OFFICE.

THE BANK OF ENGLAND, LONDON.

SIR JOHN SOANE, ARCHITECT.

THE GRÆCO-ROMAN PHASE, 1780—1820

At the beginning of the nineteenth century many people had taken advantage of the peace intervals to visit Paris and other Continental cities, and on their return to London they were disappointed with the meanness of the main London thorough-fares, which, with the exception of Whitehall, were all extremely narrow. In consequence public interest was aroused to such an extent as to result in a mania for architectural improvements. The plan of Regent's Park had been obtained from Nash in 1793, when he was architect and surveyor to the Woods and Forests, but building operations were not commenced until 1812. Nash designed many of the terraces, including Albany Street, Park Crescent, and the Park Villages. These works must be considered as examples of

FIG. 45. THE COUNTY FIRE OFFICE, REGENT STREET
John Nash and Robert Abraham, Architects

theatrical architecture ; in composition they are oftentimes extremely original, but in other respects are insincere and lack the essentials of the monumental manner.

Between the years 1813–16 Regent Street was designed and carried out under an Act of Parliament at a cost approximately of a million and a half. In the opinion of Sir Robert Smirke, nobody but the indefatigable Nash could have carried the scheme through. With the exception of two large blocks designed by Sir John Soane, Nash was responsible for the architectural design of all the buildings erected. His particular *forte* was the harmonious grouping of masses of buildings, all of which, although different in composition, produced unity of effect by being placed in juxtaposition. In 1819 he built the façade of the County Fire Office, as a termination to the eastern arm of the

Quadrant ; this front was modelled upon the design of the columnal façade to old Somerset House, designed by Inigo Jones. The planning and interior decoration of the former structure were carried out by Robert Abraham. At this date the Quadrant with the projecting colonnade was completed.

In 1832 Nash designed the twin residences in Lower Regent Street for himself and his relation Mr. Edwards, removing therefrom 29 Dover Street, which he previously refronted ; and between the years 1826–28 the United Service Club House, Pall Mall (since rebuilt), and Waterloo Place.

On account of his friendship with King George IV. he was entrusted with the building

FIG. 46. THE QUADRANT, REGENT STREET. SHOWING THE COLONNADE. *John Nash, Architect*

43

MONUMENTAL ARCHITECTURE

FIG. 47. THE QUADRANT, REGENT STREET, LOOKING TOWARDS PICCADILLY CIRCUS
John Nash, Architect

of Buckingham Palace in the years 1825–27, on the site of Buckingham House, a not ineffective design, which was subsequently marred by Blore's additions. The Marble Arch, also designed by Nash at the same date, originally stood in front of the Palace; it was removed to its present position in 1850–51. In 1828, with the assistance of his nephew, James Pennethorne, he carried out the east wing of Carlton House Terrace, and laid out St. James's Park.

Nash's other works include the County Gaol at Cardigan, 1793; the County Gaol at Hereford (Greek Doric); Highgate Archway, 1812: this structure represented an adaptation of the principle of the Roman aqueduct; and the Haymarket Theatre. The Opera House in the Haymarket was added to and altered

FIG. 48. REGENT STREET. FAÇADE ON WEST SIDE
John Nash, Architect

by Nash and George Repton in 1816–18; the Royal Arcade is the only portion of the old structure that remains standing to-day. In connection with the further improvements of the "Regency Period" a committee, called the Committee of Taste, was appointed in order to design such improvements as were imperatively required to connect the City with the West End.

FIG. 49. REGENT STREET. FAÇADE ON THE EAST SIDE
John Nash, Architect

44

THE GRÆCO-ROMAN PHASE, 1780—1820

This committee consisted of Lord Farnborough, John Wilson Croker, Sir John Soane, Sir Robert Smirke, and John Nash. The formation of Trafalgar Square, the entrance to the West Strand, and the junction between Oxford Street and Holborn were among the many improvements effected by their influence. Although John Nash was deficient in the elementary education of his profession, lacking both constructive and detail knowledge, he was a great artist, and his architecture, while it is far from faultless, is, notwithstanding, effective.

George Stanley Repton became a pupil of John Nash in 1795, and was associated with him in

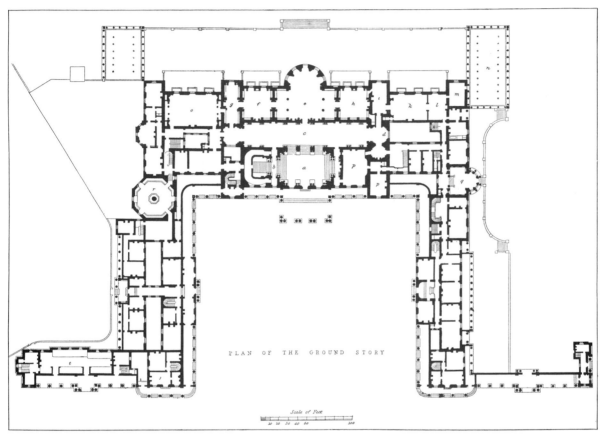

FIG. 50. BUCKINGHAM PALACE, LONDON.   GROUND PLAN   *John Nash, Architect*

1818–20. When practising together they remodelled the exterior façades of the Opera House. In 1819–20 he completed his chief work, St. Philip's Chapel, Regent Street, at a cost of £15,000. This structure was typical of the Græco-Roman school, and shows the influence of the current archæological researches abroad.* Repton left the profession after this commission, and died in 1858. There exists but scant information concerning the career of J. Johnson, who appears to have practised in Berners Street. His chief work of monumental interest is the exterior of the Mint ; the lodges and other alterations were carried out by Sir Robert Smirke. Johnson's original drawings for this building are preserved in the collection at the Royal Institute of British Architects.

To fully explain the influence of the Græco-Roman school it will be necessary to state the names and careers of six architects who at the beginning of the nineteenth century carried on the tradition in Ireland. The foremost of these distinguished men was Francis Johnston, R.H.A. A native of Ireland, he gained considerable reputation in Dublin as a Classicist of ability. In 1804 he designed the Cash Office of the Bank of Ireland, a Portland-stone interior of noble proportions and elegant detail. The General Post Office in Sackville Street, modelled on Holland's design for the East India House, was erected from his design, between the years 1815–17 ; it is carried out in Dalkey granite and Portland stone. He also added the Ionic tetrastyle portico to the south front of the

* Pulled down in 1906.

45

MONUMENTAL ARCHITECTURE

Viceregal Lodge in Phœnix Park. In 1824 he built, at his own expense, the Royal Hibernian Academy. He held the office of "Architect and Inspector of Civil Buildings" to the Board of Works in Ireland, and in this capacity designed several buildings of minor importance. Richard Johnston is supposed to be the father of Francis. The Assembly Rooms at Dublin, next to the Rotunda, are his work; they were built in 1785; at the same date he considerably improved the Rotunda by the addition of the portico and terra-cotta Wedgwood frieze under the main entablature. Robert Parke also practised chiefly in Dublin; he carried out the west colonnade to the Bank of Ireland, executed by him between the years 1787–94. In 1796–99 he designed the adjoining Commercial Buildings. The ultimate conversion of the Senate House into the Bank of Ireland was completed by him. In 1806 he designed the Royal College of Surgeons, but in 1825 it was altered and the front added by William Murray.

EAST ELEVATION

SCALE OF FEET

FIG. 51. ST. PHILIP'S CHAPEL, LOWER REGENT STREET   *George Repton, Architect*

The grand Classic tradition practised by James Gandon bore excellent results in the career of his pupil, Sir Richard Morrison, 1767–1849. After leaving Gandon, Morrison obtained an appointment in the Ordnance Department, and shortly after this was entrusted with extensive alterations to the cathedral at Cashel. At Clonmel he built the County Court House for Tipperary; and in 1812 he designed the beautiful Court House at Galway, a design which reflects the soundness of his training under Gandon. In 1816 he began the Roman Catholic Cathedral at Dublin, and in addition to these important buildings, he carried into being a considerable number of noblemen's mansions, besides adding to and remodelling others.

Probably no other architects had such scope in the South of Ireland as the brothers Pain. The Classic buildings designed by them are nearly all represented in Cork. James Pain was born in 1779 and died in 1879; his brother, George Richard, was born in 1793 and died in 1838. Both architects received their early training in the office of John Nash, and were with him during the time Regent Street was designed. Through Nash's influence they were started as architects and builders in Ireland, James practising in Limerick, while George began in Cork.

46

FIG. 52. THE MINT, TOWER HILL, LONDON. *J. Johnson, Architect*

The Lodges and alterations were carried out by Sir Robert Smirke

The most noted of their works in the monumental manner is the Cork Male Prison. This structure externally presents an appearance eminently expressive of its purpose. The Pains were thoroughly conversant with the inventions of Piranesi, as is shown by the detail of the niches on either side of the Doric portico ; moreover, they had a good conception of what constituted grand scale, and understood harmony of proportion.

George Richard Pain, unassisted by his brother, designed St. Patrick's Church, Cork, the main

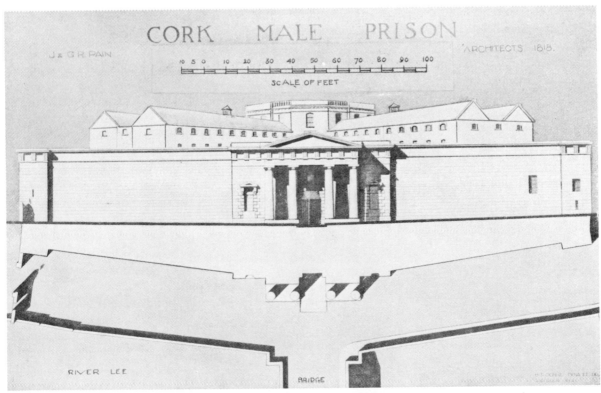

FIG. 53. *J. and G. R. Pain, Architects*

MONUMENTAL ARCHITECTURE

feature of which is the Corinthian hexastyle portico. This is contrasted by a dignified square belfry, which assists the monumental effect. The Court House is also their design, and it is

FIG. 54. THE CUSTOMS HOUSE, LONDON. ORIGINAL FAÇADE TO THE RIVER *David Laing, Architect*

distinguished for the dignity and spaciousness of the octastyle Corinthian portico, which forms the feature of main interest. The character of their buildings in general follows the work of Nash and the earlier designs of Professor C. R. Cockerell ; two of their drawings for Classic churches reflect

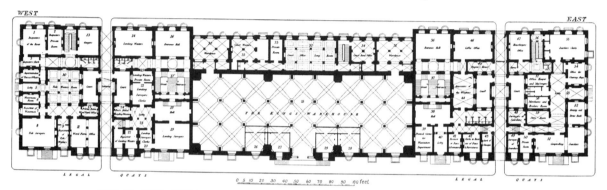

FIG. 55. THE CUSTOMS HOUSE, LONDON. PLAN OF THE GROUND FLOOR

the character of the church of All Souls, Langham Place, and St. George's Chapel, Regent Street. Various buildings in the style, some of importance and great merit, were erected from time to time by other Irish architects, but until Mulvany developed the " Neo-Grec " phase nothing remarkable was achieved.

Returning to Great Britain, it is interesting to note that the Græco-Roman school was gradually merging into a purely Greek phase. Several architects, however, continued the vernacular style, and their careers must be described.

David Laing, born in 1774, was articled to Sir John Soane. In 1810 he obtained the appointment of Architect and Surveyor of Buildings to the Board of Customs. His design for the rebuilding of the Customs House was approved about 1812. Owing to the failure of the piles under the centre portion, this part of Laing's design was pulled down and the present range of columns erected by Sir Robert Smirke. Laing's original design for the building

FIG. 56. THE CUSTOMS HOUSE, LONDON. FAÇADE TO THAMES STREET

48

was bold and striking ; the astylar centre portion relied solely on the arched fenestration for effect, and the comparative simplicity of the centre mass was contrasted by the columnar treatment assigned

to the appendages. Sir Robert Smirke's alterations to this building are, architecturally considered, no improvement on Laing's scheme. The grand façade to Thames Street exhibits a model design in brick and stone, and shows the suitability of the style for buildings of great size. Laing retired from the profession after the trouble at the Customs House, and died in 1856. The monumental manner had a worthy exponent in Robert Reid (1776–1856),who chiefly practised in the city of Edinburgh, where he

FIG. 57. THE CUSTOMS HOUSE, LEITH *Robert Reid, Architect*

erected several conspicuous buildings. Between the years 1808–40 he designed the new Courts of Law, extending round three sides of the Parliament Square ; and in the years 1811–14 he built St. George's Church in that city, terminating the vista from George Street. The latter design is a finely grouped structure designed to harmonise with the adjoining blocks of residences ; the principal feature is the dome, which is based on that of St. Paul's Cathedral. About 1812 Reid designed the Customs House at Leith, erected at a cost of £12,000, and probably the Exchange. His

contemporaries R. and J. Dickson built the Town Hall at Leith in 1828 ; the appendage is of a later date. This building was their only work in the style. The work of Robert Reid as well as that of the Dicksons shows the influence of the style practised by the brothers Adam, but it is treated in a broader manner.

Towards the close of the eighteenth century many architects published drawings of antique buildings and sculpture, and by this means contributed to the furtherance of Classic architecture. Foremost among these men were Charles Heathcote Tatham and George Ledwall Taylor.

Tatham was born in 1772,

FIG. 58. THE CUSTOMS HOUSE, GLASGOW *George Ledwall Taylor, Architect*

MONUMENTAL ARCHITECTURE

FIG. 59. THE COMMERCIAL ROOMS, BRISTOL

John Linnell Bond, Architect

and became a pupil of S. P. Cockerell. Mainly owing to the munificence of Sir John Soane, he published "Etchings of Ancient Ornamental Architecture in Rome and Italy," in three editions, 1794–95–96, followed by etchings representing fragments of Greek and Roman ornaments, folio, 1806. Many of these etchings record antique objects of art in Sir John Soane's possession, bought for him by Tatham, and at the time of publication the volumes were eagerly studied by architects and students.

George Ledwall Taylor, as an author, directed attention to the monuments of old Rome. He visited France, Italy, and Greece during the years 1817–19, and in company with John Sanders, E. Purser, and E. Cresy discovered the Lion of Chæronea. In 1821–22 Taylor and Cresy published the folio volumes "Architectural Antiquities of Rome." His architectural works include the Customs House, near Jamaica Bridge, Glasgow, a consistent trabeated design; and in 1836 he completed the east side of Trafalgar Square as flats and offices.

One of the most able Classicists of the period who practised in various parts of the country was John Linnell Bond (1766–1837), whose earlier works appear to have been erected in London. At Bristol he designed the Commercial Rooms, a charming Græco-Roman composition, which was

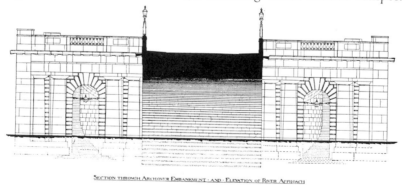

SECTION THROUGH ARCH OVER EMBANKMENT · AND · ELEVATION OF RIVER APPROACH

Scale of Feet

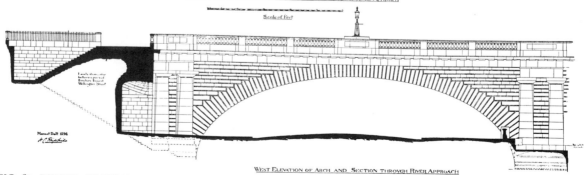

WEST ELEVATION OF ARCH AND SECTION THROUGH RIVER APPROACH

FIG. 60. DETAIL DRAWING OF WATERLOO BRIDGE. From South Kensington Museum.   *John Rennie, Architect*

completed in 1811. The interior consists of a large hall, lit by means of a circular cupola, supported by caryatides, similar in arrangement to the method of top-lighting employed by Sir John Soane in many of his buildings. Bond carried out a large coaching inn at Stamford, Lincolnshire, and possibly the design of the "Portico" in that town. He was named assistant architect with George Dodd in the Act of Parliament for the erection of the Strand, now called Waterloo Bridge, and prepared the design approved by the company. This was set aside when John Rennie took over the position of engineer for the erection of the structure. Bond was extremely clever in reconstructing such Classical compositions as the Temple of Apollo at Delphi, as well as the Temple of Jupiter at Olympia; many of his drawings of this description are now in the collection of the Royal Institute of British Architects. His travels abroad included a tour through Greece and Italy, which he made in 1818, and from which he returned to England in 1821. Although his completed works were few in number, his taste and ability considerably advanced the Neo-Classic move-

FIG. 61. WATERLOO BRIDGE AND SOMERSET HOUSE. SHOWING COMPOSITION OF THE TWO STRUCTURES

ment. At this period architectural design was not considered to be solely the province of the architect, and in this connection the names of three prominent engineers need to be included.

The foremost is John Rennie (1761–1821). Primarily a civil engineer of world-renowned ability, none will deny his prowess as an architect; all his architectural structures have the distinguishing characteristics of the monumental, firmness and solidity. Rennie had a great reputation as a builder of bridges; in the early part of his career he built the bridge at Kelso, which anticipated by some years his design for Waterloo Bridge. The architectural *motif* for this structure was a projecting pylon, formed of the Roman Doric order, placed on the starlings between each bay; the semicircular wing terminations are also similar in design to those at Waterloo Bridge. The graceful design for Southwark Bridge, which spans the Thames between Queenhithe and Bankside by three colossal arches, is further evidence of his daring as an engineer, and proves his refined taste as an architect; it was completed and opened for traffic in 1819. Waterloo Bridge consists of nine equal semi-elliptic arches, each of 120 feet in span, with a rise of 34 feet 6 inches. The whole of the arches and the exterior face of the bridge are built of granite from the Cornish quarries at Penryn; the total cost of the work when finished, including the land and approaches, amounted to £1,050,000. The selection of the Greek Doric order as a *motif* of architectural expression was extremely happy. The nature of the building material prevented the use of minute detail, and in consequence the impressiveness of the structure was enhanced by the simplicity of the mouldings. The bridge and approaches were completed and opened with great ceremony in 1817 by George IV., then Prince Regent. The design for London Bridge was also made by John Rennie, but no detailed working drawings or specification were prepared by him.

*

FIG. 62. WATERLOO BRIDGE. WING TREATMENT. *John Rennie, Architect*

His son, afterwards Sir John Rennie, erected the structure from the original design, and it was finished in 1831. Sir John Rennie had many architects as his friends, including his brother-in-law, Professor C. R. Cockerell, and Sir Robert Smirke. When the question of approaches to New London Bridge came to be considered he obtained a scheme from Cockerell and exhibited it to the managing committee. It was, however, considered to be too costly, although in reality it would have proved the right idea for the importance of the situation. The committee referred the matter to Sir Robert Smirke, then one of the Crown architects, and he designed the present buildings on both sides of the bridge, as far as King William Street on the north and the old Town Hall of Southwark on the south. These buildings were considered by Sir John Rennie to be unworthy of their author.

William Tierney Clark (1783–1852) was a civil engineer of conspicuous architectural capability.

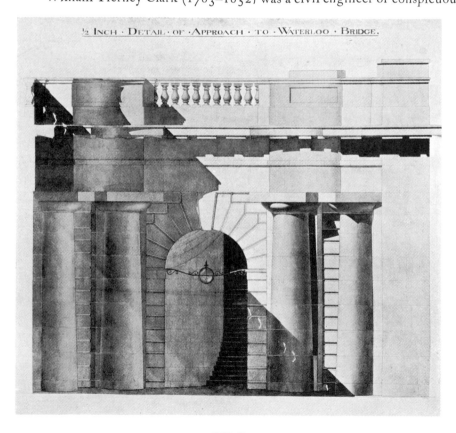

FIG. 63.

Born at Bristol, he was apprenticed at an early age to a millwright, afterwards being engaged at the Coalbrookdale Iron-works. Sir John Rennie discovered him there in 1808, and offered him a position of responsibility at his Holland Street works, afterwards entrusting him with the superintendence of some of his most important work.

In 1824 he commenced the construction of Hammersmith Suspension Bridge, noted at the time for the design of the pylons carrying the chains; it was removed in 1885 to make way for the present structure. His chief monumental work was the bridge

THE GRÆCO-ROMAN PHASE, 1780—1820

built for the Duke of Norfolk over the Adur at Shoreham. In this design the architectural interest centres in the adaptation of a triumphal arch *motif* to the engineering problem. The whole structure is conceived with rare taste and skill, even to the design of the toll-house on the Shoreham side of the river.

The Rennies, father and son, and William Tierney Clark were the last members of the old order of architect-engineers who were really capable of extending their labours to æsthetic problems. From an architectural point of view the Classic spirit, as interpreted during the eighteenth century, practically continued until the first quarter of the nineteenth, when the influence of the purity of Hellenic *motifs* became more apparent. The Greek phase, however, was purely a transitionary one which led to a broader acceptance of Classic principles of design. Although many of the public buildings erected during this phase show little or no regard for warmth of character, they were scholarly to a degree and always accord with the first principles of academic composition. The exponents of the Greek phase, in their desire to arrive at instantaneous perfection, devoted their whole attention to the transplantation of Hellenic forms from Greece to England, and while they maintained a high standard of taste they did not advance creative activity among architects. Yet a study of the architecture of this period is of supreme importance, because it formed the foundation for the school of Cockerell, Elmes, and Barry.

FOUNTAIN IN THE PUMP ROOM, PITVILLE SPA, CHELTENHAM

53

CHAPTER IV

THE GREEK PHASE, 1820–1840

WILLIAM WILKINS—GANDY-DEERING—SIR ROBERT SMIRKE—WILLIAM
BROOKS—GEORGE SMITH—DECIMUS BURTON—JOHN PAPWORTH—HENRY
GOODRIDGE—FRANCIS GOODWIN—CHARLES FOWLER—LEWIS VULLIAMY—
JOHN FOSTER—ARCHIBALD ELLIOT—DAVID HAMILTON—THOMAS HAMIL-
TON—WILLIAM BURN—WILLIAM HENRY PLAYFAIR—CLARKE AND BELL

VIEWED from the standpoint of architectural development, the early years of the nineteenth
century, from the initiation of the Regency in 1811 until the accession of Queen Victoria
in 1837, constitute a period in the national history which demands close attention. The
tremendous upheaval occasioned by the Napoleonic wars, which swept Europe from Madrid
to Moscow, had practically excluded Englishmen from intercourse with the Continent. Barred from
France and Italy, English artists travelled by the long sea route to Athens and the seaports of Asia
Minor, to augment their previous researches by a scientific study of the arts of Greece. The amateur
even at this comparatively late date was extremely active in his endeavours to advance artistic taste,
Thomas Hope of Deepdene and Lord Elgin being most prominent in this connection, the former
by his publications and patronage of artists and the latter by his acquisition of the famous Elgin
Marbles. Sixty years had lapsed since the first volume of Stuart's "Antiquities of Athens" had
appeared, and during the intervening period a greater knowledge concerning Hellenic art had been
circulated. In addition public opinion had slowly but surely been veering round in favour of the
purity and refinement of Greek architecture. The finest works associated with the names of the
brothers Adam during the late eighteenth century exhibit the prevailing desire to emulate the chaste
beauty of Greek ornament ; the Græco-Roman phase in all its workings was but the outcome of an
intensification of this desire. The commendable labours of Holland, Soane, and the Wyatts prepared
the way for the monumental works of Smirke, Wilkins, and Hamilton, and later for the brilliant
culmination. In the attainments of such sculptors as Nollekens, Flaxman, Chantrey, and Westmacott
the value of a "Greek" standard of excellence had long been appreciated ; and in the circles of
fashionable society the affection for dilettantism raged as furiously as ever. Artists, architects, and
sculptors were among the members of the Dilettanti Society at this period, and in consequence research
work became an essential feature in an artist's education. The enthusiasm for refinement in architecture and the kindred arts grew apace, and though excess of zeal prompted some exponents of
"Greek" to literally reproduce the temple frontals of Greece, on the whole the development was
steady. Another factor which to some extent militated against the furtherance of the Greek phase
was the imaginary ambidexterity of those architects who tried to design both in the Gothic and
Classic manner.

The termination of the Napoleonic wars in 1815, occasioned to England an increased prosperity
and relief from Napoleon's "Continental system." As a result a great building epoch commenced ;
the seaside towns on the east and south coasts sprang up from a collection of fishing-villages. The
inland watering-places, such as Harrogate, Buxton, Leamington, and Cheltenham, were extended
practically to their present size. Eighteenth-century London burst its bounds : Regent's Park was
laid out and the squares of Belgravia were erected ; and gradually the outlying villages were
absorbed to form part of the Metropolis. Similar town-planning expansions were taking place in
all the principal towns of the United Kingdom. Edinburgh, already renowned for its "New Town,"
witnessed further changes. Dublin was extended by the creation of Kingstown, and Bristol was
expanded by the building of Clifton. Under the direction of Telford the main trunk roads were
immensely improved, and travelling facilities thereby increased. The age of steam dawned, to
extend the commercial enterprise of the country ; harbours and engineering works unprecedented
in extent were undertaken. Many young architects who had been travelling in Greece and the
East to complete their studies returned home to find their services in immediate demand. In

THE GREEK PHASE, 1820—1840

consequence by the year 1820 the Greek phase was firmly established in England, to react to a great extent on the architecture of Europe and America. Yet only a quarter of a century separates this period of activity from the age of Pitt and the French Revolution.

The Greek school had no more learned exponent than William Wilkins, R.A. (1778–1839), a fastidious scholar and man of refined taste. In 1801 he was nominated at the University of Cambridge Travelling Bachelor, and travelled for four years in Greece, Asia Minor, and Italy, publishing in 1807 "Antiquities of Magna Græcia," a translation of Vitruvius, 1812, and "Prolusiones Architectonicæ," 1827–37. In 1837 Wilkins was appointed Professor of Architecture at the Royal Academy, but did not lecture. In 1806 he designed Haileybury College, in Hertfordshire, for the East India Company. Between the years 1806–11 he carried out two sides of Downing College, at a cost of £60,000, and in 1808 he designed the Greek Doric pillar in

FIG. 64. UNIVERSITY COLLEGE, GOWER STREET. ELEVATION OF MAIN FAÇADE
William Wilkins, R.A., and Gandy-Deering, R.A., Architects

Sackville Street, Dublin, as a monument to Nelson. In 1809 he erected Grange Park, Hampshire, on the site of an older house designed by Inigo Jones. Another monumental pillar to Nelson was designed by Wilkins and erected at Yarmouth in 1817. Between the years 1808–10 he added the Doric entrance to the Kingston Rooms at Bath ; after the fire of 1820 this structure was rebuilt as a Royal Literary Institution, with the exception of the portico, which was retained. On several occasions he competed against Cockerell, Rickman, and Burton, with varying success. After 1822 he was associated with Gandy-Deering on several important works. Their joint design for a monument 280 feet high commemorating Waterloo was selected by the Committee of Taste, and a model exhibited at the Royal Academy. In 1822–26 with Gandy-Deering he designed the University Club House, Pall Mall East, which was demolished in 1906 ; this building is one of the finest structures connected with his name. With Gandy-Deering he erected the new University College in Gower Street during the years 1827–28. His personal works include St. George's Hospital, Hyde Park Corner, completed 1827–28, and the National Gallery, which he finished in 1838. Wilkins as a monumental architect was not a strong man ; he had great opportunities, but failed to deal with them satisfactorily. He was an accomplished draughtsman and an archæologist of considerable reputation, but unfortunately he did not possess the elastic mind nor requisite power

MONUMENTAL ARCHITECTURE

of adaptation essential to a first-class designer, and his work in consequence appears unsympathetic. Wilkins must have felt very sensitive on this point himself, for he strove to impart interesting silhouettes to University College and the National Gallery by introducing superfluous domical features. The central portico to the former building, with its admirable arrangement of steps, is the finest Classic portico in England, but the junction it makes with the wings is far from happy. The two sides of the open quadrangle are relieved by projections with effective semicircular bays, which are intended to be viewed in relation to the central feature.* The main front to the National

FIG. 65. EXETER HALL, STRAND, 1830–31
Gandy-Deering, Architect

Gallery is likewise distinguished by an effective portico and well-arranged steps, but the relation of this feature to the whole front is disproportionate. Wilkins was much handicapped in this design by having to use some of the columns and capitals from Carlton House. The straggling main front of the building is not grand enough in composition to head such an important place as Trafalgar Square, but when viewed from Pall Mall the component masses coalesce and the general effect is better. He never erred on the side of coarse detail ; his mouldings and ornaments are invariably beautiful, and well selected for the purposes they serve.

His colleague, John Peter Gandy-Deering, R.A. (1787–1850), had a far greater power for assimilating and transmuting the *motifs* of antiquity. After spending some time in the office of James Wyatt, he was sent by the Society of Dilettanti with their second mission to Greece, where he remained during the years 1811–13, with Sir W. Gell, F. Bedford, and G. Walter. The results of this expedition are given in the Society's " Unedited Antiquities of Attica," London, 1817. In 1817–19 he contributed the text to " Pompeiana," published with Sir William Gell. This work was much appreciated by Hittorff, who translated it into French in 1827. As before mentioned, Gandy-Deering was associated with Wilkins in the design of the University Club House and University College, Gower Street. In 1825 he designed St. Mark's Church, in North Audley Street, a refined and original building, which was finished in 1828. One of his most brilliant designs was the exterior to Exeter Hall, built between the years 1830–31, at a cost of £30,000, and pulled down in 1907. This façade was a complete vindication of the development of Greek architectural forms for a modern street-front. The Lysicrates Corinthian order was placed distyle *in antis* as the main feature of the building, and by this simple procedure the architect evolved a design eminently suited to the narrow site. The Pimlico Institution, in Ebury Street, was built in 1830. Gandy-Deering was distinguished for the originality and purity of his compositions, as well as for his thorough knowledge of the antique.

The next architect of importance in relation to the development is Sir Robert Smirke, R.A. (1781–1867), who during the first quarter of the nineteenth century had the largest practice in London. At the age of fifteen he entered the office of Sir John Soane for one year, afterwards becoming a pupil of a surveyor named Bush. In 1796 he gained admittance to the Royal Academy Schools, winning the Gold Medal in 1799. Following the custom of the day, he left England in 1801 for a prolonged tour abroad, and during his travels visited Holland, Paris, Rome, Naples,

* These features were erected at a later date.

Plate XXV.

THE ART GALLERY, MANCHESTER.

SIR CHARLES BARRY, ARCHITECT.

THE NATIONAL GALLERY, LONDON. EAST ELEVATION.

WILLIAM WILKINS, R.A., ARCHITECT.

Plate XXVI.

THE BRITISH MUSEUM, LONDON. DETAIL OF PORTICO.

SIR ROBERT SMIRKE, R.A. ARCHITECT. 1825-1847.

Athens, and Sicily. Although a large number of his domestic buildings were conceived in an affected version of the mediæval castellated style, for which the sentiment of the day was responsible, his public structures reflect the rigid Classic discipline then in vogue for civic architecture. His monumental works comprise some of the most important public buildings in the kingdom. Not content with the mere transcription of any of the Classic orders, he achieved original combinations of primary masses in all his designs. Generally speaking, his favourite order was the Greek Ionic. Having designed the exterior of a building in the monumental manner, he seems to have lost sight of the necessity for such architectural embellishments as groups of sculpture and other ornamental features, which in this country are

FIG. 66. THE BRITISH MUSEUM, LONDON. MAIN STAIRCASE
Sir R. Smirke, R.A., Architect

essential aids to architectural expression. His greatest work was the rebuilding of the British Museum, the east wing of which, including the King's Library, he carried out between the years 1825–28. The south front of the structure was practically finished in 1847. The General Post Office,

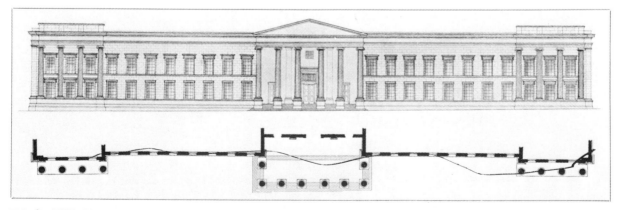

FIG. 67. THE GENERAL POST OFFICE, ST. MARTIN'S-LE-GRAND
Sir R. Smirke, R.A., Architect

MONUMENTAL ARCHITECTURE

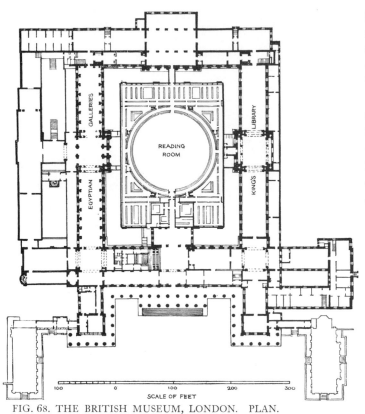

FIG. 68. THE BRITISH MUSEUM, LONDON. PLAN.
Sir R. Smirke, R.A., Architect

St. Martin's-le-Grand, was built between the years 1824–29, and the College of Physicians, with the Union Club House forming the west side of Trafalgar Square, between the years 1824–27. In 1825 he built Belgrave Chapel, in Belgrave Square, which has been recently pulled down. The Council House at Bristol is perhaps his most ornate building. This stands on a corner site, and reveals Smirke's ability to impart monumental dignity to a comparatively small building. When the centre portion of the London Customs House showed signs of defective construction Sir Robert Smirke was called upon to remedy the defects ; he accordingly pulled down the original centre portion and substituted the present façade, consisting of a range of columns. Between the years 1830–31 he completed the river-front of Somerset House and built King's College to form the east wing. His other important works include the New United Service Club (now the Junior United), Pall Mall ; Covent Garden Theatre, which he

FIG. 69. THE UNION CLUB HOUSE AND COLLEGE OF PHYSICIANS, TRAFALGAR SQUARE
Sir R. Smirke, R.A., Architect

Plate XXVII.

THE BRITISH MUSEUM, LONDON. THE KING'S LIBRARY.

SIR ROBERT SMIRKE, R.A. ARCHITECT. 1825-1847.

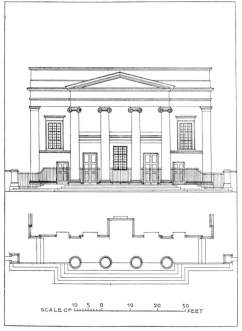

FIG. 70. BELGRAVE CHAPEL. S.W.

FIG. 71. THE COLLEGE OF PHYSICIANS, 1824–27

rebuilt in the years 1808–9 ; the Equitable Assurance Company's offices, Bridge Street, Blackfriars, built in 1829 ; the offices of the Duchy of Lancaster, and Lancaster Place, Waterloo Bridge ; St. Mary's Church, Bryanston Square, 1823–24. He designed the Wellington Monument at Dublin in 1817 ; the latter is a magnificent obelisk terminating the vista looking up the river Liffey. He erected the buildings adjoining Exeter Hall (now demolished) in the Strand in 1830–31, Hoare's Bank, in Fleet Street, in 1838, and between the years 1824–40 façades to the north and south approaches to

London Bridge, as well as those to King William Street and Moorgate Street. Alterations to the Royal Mint on Tower Hill, and other buildings in the Temple and Chancery Lane, were also erected from his designs. Many architects of subsequent renown served as pupils in his office ; among these were his brother, Sydney Smirke, C. R. Cockerell, H. Roberts, J. Kay, W. Burn, L. Vulliamy, and C. C. Nelson. Sir Robert Smirke's influence on the development of the Greek phase of monumental architecture was very considerable, especially in the architectural decoration of interiors. In many of his later works, until his retirement in 1845, he had the assistance of his brother, Sydney Smirke.

While Sir John Soane and Sir Robert Smirke were occupying the attention of the public with their own version of the monumental manner, the Inwoods (father and sons) remained practically unnoticed. The family consisted of William Inwood, the father (1771–1843), Henry William Inwood, F.S.A. (1794–1843), and Charles Frederick Inwood (1798–1840).

The professional career of these architects was so intimately connected that for the purpose of describing their important works they will be

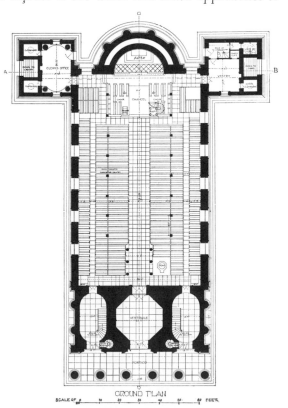

FIG. 72. ST. PANCRAS CHURCH. PLAN. 1819–22

MONUMENTAL ARCHITECTURE

regarded as one firm. The dominant spirit who influenced their style was the eldest son, Henry William Inwood. He spent some time at Athens during the years 1818–19, studying the Athenian antiquities, and on his return he published the result of his researches in a folio volume under the title "The Erechtheion at Athens," with marble and terra-cotta fragments of Athenian architecture. Between July 1819 and May 1822 the firm designed and built St. Pancras New Church, Euston Square. This structure is a remarkable recombination of Greek *motifs*, including the caryatide tribune and Ionic order from the eastern portico of the Erechtheion. From the date of its completion this beautiful building has been subjected to

FIG. 73. THE LONDON INSTITUTION, FINSBURY CIRCUS   *William Brooks, Architect*

mischievous and ill-considered attack, mainly because its critics have been unable to realise the elementary principles of academic design. In a masterly manner the Inwoods applied the refinement of the Periclean age of Athenian architecture to the design of a parish church, with results of lasting value to architectural taste. The chief building material used for the structure is Portland stone, with cast terra-cotta enrichments by Rossi. Their other works in the style were the Camden Chapel, Pratt Street, Camden Town, built between the years 1822–24, and that in Regent Square, built in the years 1824–26.

Little is known concerning the career of the accomplished William Brooks beyond the fact that he was probably a pupil of George Maddox. In 1815 he was awarded the first premium for the design of the London Institution, which he erected between the years 1815–19.* The principal front to Finsbury Circus is reminiscent of Sir John Soane's academic manner, and this is more especially apparent in the application of the Græco-Roman Corinthian order, from the Temple of Vesta at Tivoli, for the principal storey. The site presented many difficulties which were successfully overcome by the architect. The chief feature in the interior arrangement of the building is the library on the first floor, 97 feet in length by 42 in width, and 28 feet high, a perfectly proportioned

* The original Perspective Drawing showing a dome is in the Library of the London Institution.

60

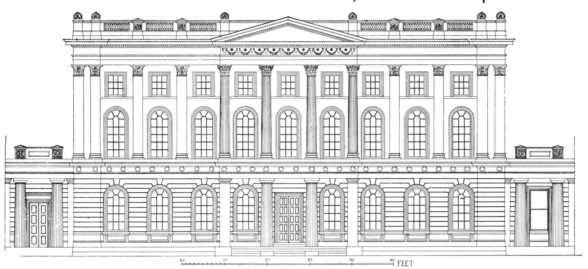

FIG. 74. THE LONDON INSTITUTION, FINSBURY CIRCUS. MAIN ELEVATION   *William Brooks, Architect*

room with beautiful appointments. The Lecture Theatre is ingeniously connected with the main portion of the building by means of an octagonal vestibule placed in juxtaposition to the principal staircase ; and this fine room provides accommodation for 600 persons. The rooms immediately behind the lecture table are used as laboratories. Not only does the plan show a remarkable directness and simplicity in arrangement, but it also demonstrates the theory of axiality as applied to an asymmetrical building. Brooks also designed and erected the Finsbury Chapel, Moorfields ; and the design of the Doric Church at Stoke Newington is attributed to his skill.

The Greek phase was productive of many architects of minor renown who laboured incessantly to advance architectural taste. In regard to the career and works of George Smith (1783–1869), there is to be seen a continuance of the late eighteenth-century traditions blended with the newer teaching of Smirke and Soane. After spending five years, from 1797 to 1802, as a pupil in the office of Robert Furze Brettingham, at No. 9 Berkeley Square, in 1802 George

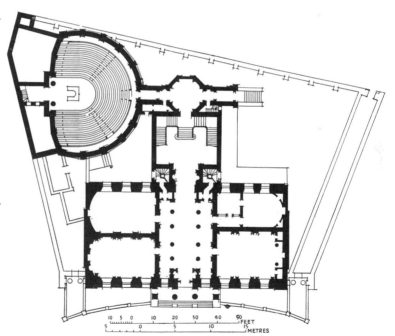

FIG. 75. THE LONDON INSTITUTION. PLAN.   *William Brooks, Architect*

Smith left him to assist James Wyatt, and subsequently D. Alexander and C. Beazley. His monumental buildings were the new stone tower and entrance to the Royal Exchange, and reparations to that structure, which he carried out between the years 1820–25, and which were eventually destroyed by fire ; the London Corn Exchange, Mark Lane, built in 1827–28 ; the Town Hall and Court House, St. Albans, 1829, at a cost of £6991, and many houses in that city. In 1823 he built St. Paul's Schools, St. Paul's Churchyard, which were pulled down in 1885. His manner represented a broad handling of Greek detail blended with the vernacular style of the day. It is evident from his buildings that he had studied the details of Greek and Roman architecture in no niggardly fashion ; this is to be seen in his daringly original design for the Corn Exchange and

61

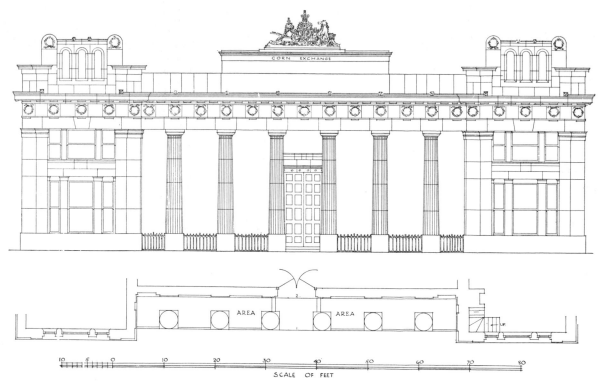

FIG. 76. THE CORN EXCHANGE, MARK LANE, 1827-28.   ELEVATION AND PLAN.   *George Smith, Architect*

FIG. 77. THE CORN EXCHANGE, MARK LANE, 1827-28   *George Smith, Architect*

Plate XXVIII.

WEST ELEVATION.

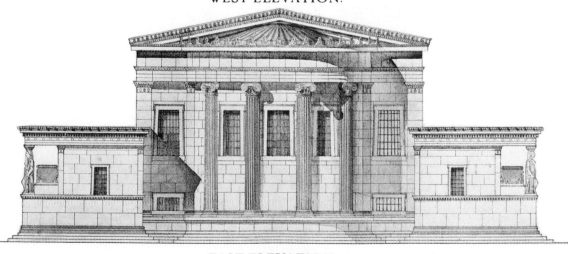

EAST ELEVATION.
ST. PANCRAS CHURCH, LONDON.
THE INWOODS, ARCHITECTS. 1819-1822.

Plate XXIX.

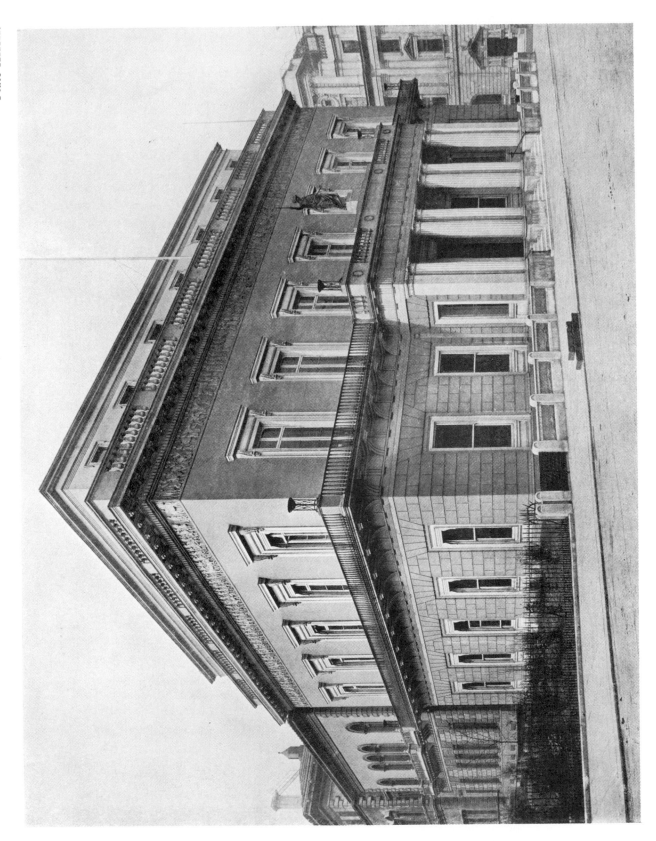

THE ATHENÆUM CLUB, PALL MALL, LONDON.

DECIMUS BURTON, ARCHITECT, 1829–30.

THE GREEK PHASE, 1820—1840

the employment of the order from the Temple of Vesta at Tivoli as the main *motif* for the façade of St. Paul's Schools. He held several appointments in London, being surveyor to the Mercers Company, the Coopers' Company, and the Gresham Commission, designing Gresham College as well as being surveyor to the trustees of Morden College.

The career of the talented Decimus Burton was of great importance to the development of Classic architecture. This distinguished architect was born in the year 1800, and survived until 1881; therefore, while his early life and work coincided with the period of the Regency, his later years were contemporary with the various abortive revivals which took place during the last quarter of the nineteenth century. He was the tenth son of James Burton, one of the most successful speculative builders of the day, who designed the streets and squares forming the northern part of Bloomsbury. His architectural training was received partly in the office of George Maddox and partly in that of his father. The former was an accomplished designer, and very materially assisted young Burton to form his taste for the finesse of Greek architecture. In 1869 Burton presented an album of drawings by George Maddox to the collection of the Royal Institute of British Architects. At the age of twenty-one he entered into active practice, and designed several private houses in Regent's Park, including The Holme, a residence for his father. Clarence Terrace and Cornwall Terrace are also attributed to him; of these the latter is the most successful in composition. In 1831 he designed and erected Charing Cross Hospital, with a fine feature facing the Strand; and about the same period he designed club premises in Lower Regent Street, which are now occupied by a stores company.

During the early years of his career the opportunity for foreign travel did not present itself, although later in life he visited both Greece and Italy. Taking this into consideration, the scholarly character of his work is all the more remarkable, and shows the thoroughness of the training afforded to a young student by the Royal Academy Schools of that day. The Colosseum in Regent's Park, commenced in 1825 and demolished in 1875, was his first monumental work; this consisted of a Greek version of the Roman Pantheon *motif*, very skilfully adapted. His reputation, however, rests chiefly on the architectural features he designed for the Government at Hyde Park and Constitution Hill. His finest work is undoubtedly the Athenæum Club, Pall Mall, which was opened in 1830; even the addition of the modern attic storey failed to destroy the classic beauty of this building. Decimus

FIG. 78. ARCH ON CONSTITUTION HILL. FROM BURTON'S DRAWING AT THE ROYAL INSTITUTE OF BRITISH ARCHITECTS, SHOWING QUADRIGA ORIGINALLY INTENDED

63

MONUMENTAL ARCHITECTURE

Burton anticipated Barry's "astylar" treatment by boldly reserving the order for the entrance portico alone ; the attachment of this feature to the basement storey is the least successful part of the design which the projecting balcony, prominent as it is, fails to unify satisfactorily. The architect demonstrated in this design that mass alone is of importance to monumental effect, and to substantiate his theory he arranged the sculptured ornament and other sub-*motifs* in broad symmetrical groups. The structure next to be considered is the dignified triumphal arch terminating Constitution Hill, a Roman design with Greek detail. The relative scale of the arch and the bronze quadriga Burton intended as a crowning feature is shown by his original water-colour drawing now at the Royal Institute of British Architects. The Ionic archway and screen at Hyde Park Corner, although correct in massing, displays inherent weaknesses in the design of the three constituent arched openings. In each instance the distance between the columns is too great for the entablature to span, as well as being out of rhythm with the columns forming the screen. The lodges at Hyde Park Corner, Stanhope Gate, and Grosvenor Gate, as well as the colonnade to the Arsenal, are instances of his sound adaptation of the Greek Doric order for buildings of small scale. Mention must also be made of his ability as a designer of such minor features as gates, piers, and railings, which show Greek ornamental features.

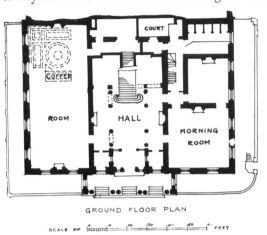

FIG. 79. THE ATHENÆUM CLUB, PALL MALL. PLAN.   *Decimus Burton, Architect*

Burton's ability for town-planning from the year 1830 onwards was in great demand. He carried out extensive schemes at Tunbridge Wells, Brighton, St. Leonards, and Hastings, nearly all the terraces and squares designed by him being similiar in character to those built at Regent's Park and in other parts of London.

At the beginning of the nineteenth century John B. Papworth (1775–1847) was one of the leading spirits of the Neo-Classic movement, and led the school of architectural professors in matters of ornamental design. Unfortunately his talents were limited to building mansions for the nobility and gentry, as well as modernising and embellishing existing houses. In 1823 he opened up the north elevation of St. Bride's Church, Fleet Street, which had previously been shut out from view. This he achieved by forming "St. Bride's Avenue," consisting of a series of houses and shops with an opening between them, thereby allowing the steeple of St. Bride's to form the climax to the vista. His influence was experienced by many architects, sculptors, and painters, and as an essayist on matters of art and design he wielded great power. Between the years 1825–30 his services were requisitioned to plan and survey the existing properties for the purpose of forming a proposed "London Central Street," in continuation northwards from the Fleet Market, and the proposed "Greshambury New Street," from Cheapside into Queen Street. These schemes were not carried into execution at the time, although at a later date they were partially realised. Papworth's versatility was extraordinary ; from an early period his talents were in request by clients and tradespeople for furniture and other designs, and he was in no small degree responsible for the English version of the "Empire style." Not content with the pedantic reproduction of conventional Greek ornament, he mastered its spirit, and in his own work he demonstrated the amazing tractability of Hellenistic art. George Papworth, his third son, carried out numerous works in Ireland, the most important in the monumental manner being the King's Bridge over the river Liffey, which he built between the years 1823–27.

While the Greek school were gaining adherents in London many architects practising in the provinces were not slow to take advantage of the Academic movement, and a vast number of creditable monumental buildings were erected in various parts of the country. Prominent among the latter men was Henry Edmund Goodridge (1797–1865), who enjoyed considerable reputation as an able Classicist. He practised chiefly in the city of Bath, erecting in 1821 a new Ionic façade to the Independent Chapel, and in 1825 the monumental tower called Lansdown Tower, as a retreat

Plate XXX.

THE LANSDOWN TOWER, BATH.

HENRY EDMUND GOODRIDGE, ARCHITECT. 1825.

for Beckford, the author of " Vathek." The Byzantine entrance gateway was added in 1845. In the same year he built the arcade called the Corridor, in 1827 Bathwick or Cleveland Bridge and the houses forming the approaches. The external stone staircase and terracing which form the glory of Prior Park were designed by Goodridge in 1829. About this time he added the spacious dormitories, the theatre, and the observatory, as well as the chapel.

In 1829 he made the first of several tours in Italy, sketching among the ruins of the Forum, there meeting Sir William Tite. This visit had a very decided effect on his later work, which is noticeable in the character of his two villas, Monte Bello and Fiesole. Goodridge numbered amongst his professional friends Sir John Soane and Professor Thomas Leverton Donaldson, and for many years he carried on a considerable correspondence with these eminent men. Like every other Classic architect of the day, he relied on an extensive collection of architectural books of reference, including a number of volumes of Piranesi's etchings, Wilkins's " Magna Græcia," and Canina's restoration of Roman buildings, to all of which he constantly referred. His greatest achievement in the monumental manner is the Lansdown Tower, which measures 154 feet in height to the top of the lantern. In this design Goodridge displayed his genius for original Classic composition, and while

FIG. 80. PRIOR PARK, BATH. THE TERRACING   *H. E. Goodridge, Architect*

he accepted a Greek *motif* for the culminating feature, in this instance the Choragic monument of Lysicrates, he transposed it to suit the conditions of his design. His son assisted him in many of his later works. Harvey Lonsdale Elmes was for some time his assistant, and after he had won the competition for St. George's Hall at Liverpool he acknowledged the excellent Classic training he had received from Goodridge.

The monumental buildings erected by Francis Goodwin (1784–1835) are comparatively few. This is mainly accounted for by his practice being chiefly an ecclesiastical one. The old Town Hall and Assembly Rooms at Manchester, which were erected between the years 1822–24, and recently demolished, are regarded as his chief work, especially the fine character of the interior. He had a preference for the Greek Ionic order, which he used with discrimination and knowledge. At Macclesfield, in the years 1823–24, he built the Assembly Rooms and Town Hall, and in 1824 the County Prison at Derby. Goodwin's Classic buildings are typical of the high-class work at that time proceeding in all parts of the country. Oftentimes the architects responsible for the important buildings in provincial towns were men of comparative obscurity, yet such was the enthusiasm for scholarly architecture that even at a remote distance from London the new buildings were equal in merit to any that enriched the Metropolis.

Another architect whose taste was devoted to the fastidious refinement of the Classic movement was Charles Fowler (1792–1867). His first experience of architecture was gained in the office of an Exeter surveyor. On the completion of his apprenticeship he came to London, about the year 1814; and entered the office of D. S. Laing as an assistant, afterwards taking up professional practice for himself. Covent Garden Market is his best achievement. This was completed in 1830, after which he commenced in the year 1831 Hungerford Market,* pulled down to make way for Hungerford Bridge; and in 1836 he carried out the lower or Western Market in Exeter. He also directed his

* Two water-colour views of Hungerford Market are contained in the library of the Royal Institute of British Architects.

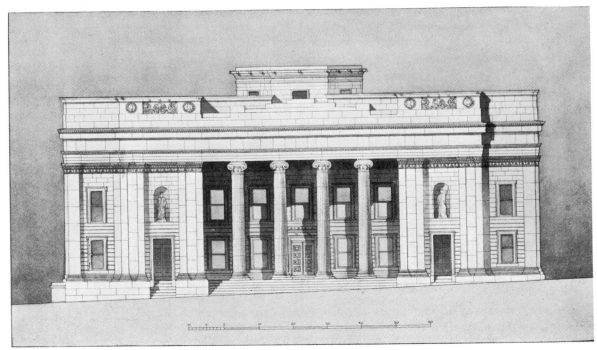

FIG. 81. THE OLD TOWN HALL, MANCHESTER, 1822–24   *Francis Goodwin, Architect*

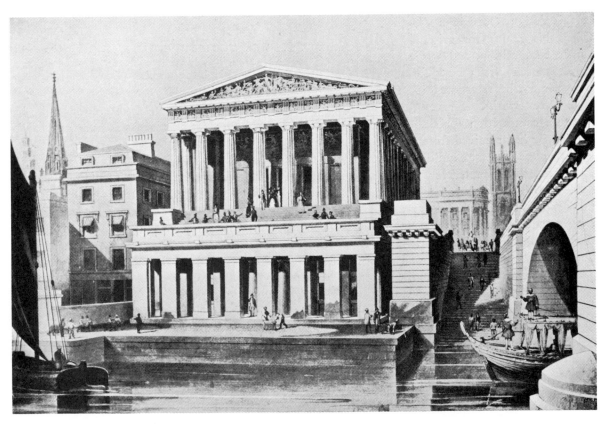

FIG. 82. A PRELIMINARY DESIGN FOR THE FISHMONGERS' HALL, LONDON BRIDGE

attention to the design of bridges, competing in 1822 for the design of London Bridge, in which he gained the first premium, but was not employed to execute the work. In 1826 he carried out the bridge over the Dart at Totnes, and probably designed the houses near that structure. Among his pupils was Henry Roberts, who afterwards entered the office of Sir R. Smirke. The only building designed by Roberts in the monumental manner is the hall of the Fishmongers' Company, erected between the years 1831–33. A preliminary design for the building is shown by the accompanying illustration. The edifice as erected is distinguished by its simplicity and harmonic relation to the design of London Bridge, and in this regard it is an improvement on the buildings opposite,

designed by Sir Robert Smirke. The elevation to the river is the best portion of the structure, and most appropriate to its situation ; the composition of the east front resembles the side elevation of the Union Club House in Trafalgar Square. The Fishmongers' Hall is one of the few buildings in London that can be viewed from a distance without losing definition in its detail : the light and shade resulting from the simple disposition of the horizontal and vertical elements is very effective,

FIG. 83. THE FISHMONGERS' HALL, LONDON BRIDGE. FROM THE RIVER.
Henry Roberts, Architect

and if there is a paucity of idea displayed in the selection of the ornamental features it is atoned for by the excellence of the whole composition.

The career of Lewis Vulliamy (1790–1871) rightly belongs to the period of the culmination, but as the majority of his designs were erected during the Greek phase and under the influence of the contemporary school they must be considered as forming a part of this transitionary period.

After spending some years as a pupil in the office of Sir Robert Smirke he obtained the Royal Academy Gold Medal in 1813, and the travelling studentship in 1818, proceeding thence abroad. He was away in Italy and Greece as well as Asia Minor for four years. On his return to London in 1821 he settled down to practise, and obtained an extensive professional connection. The first of his works, namely, the Law Institution in Chancery Lane, he completed between the years 1830–36. In 1838 he rebuilt the façade of the Royal Institution in Albemarle Street. Dorchester House, Park Lane, erected from his designs between 1848–57, belongs to the period of the culmination, and this mansion is rightly considered to be his masterpiece. With regard to the latter structure, the arrangement of the house with the entrance courtyard and enclosing walls presents one of the finest instances of town-planning in London, not only for the grandeur of its plan, but for the beauty of the accessory details. His brother, George Vulliamy (1817–86), became a pupil of Sir Charles Barry for five years. During the years 1841–43 he travelled in Greece, Asia Minor, and Egypt. He designed, among other works as architect to the Board of Works, the lamp standards on the Thames Embankment and the large ones in Northumberland Avenue, also the pedestal and sphinxes to Cleopatra's Needle.

Another architect of this day who achieved renown was John Foulston, who became a prolific worker in the style and author of " Public Buildings erected in the West of England," published in 1838. He was born in 1772, and at an early age became a pupil of Thomas Hardwick, under whom he gained an extensive knowledge of Classic architecture. He first secured fame as an architect in 1811, when he obtained the award for a design for the buildings at Plymouth comprising the Royal Hotel, the Assembly Rooms, and theatre. After this commission he took up his residence in Plymouth, and speedily became the leading architect in the district. His influence extended beyond his architectural practice, and his career must be regarded as the prime factor in the subsequent art movement in the South-west of England. When Foulston first settled in Plymouth

FIG. 84. DORCHESTER HOUSE, PARK LANE, 1848-57   *Lewis Vulliamy, Architect*

there were few buildings worthy the title of " Classic." The result of his enthusiasm fired a desire in others for the architectural betterment of Plymouth, Devonport, and Torquay, and for this reason alone his name will long be remembered.

In the works of John Foster (1786–1846) is to be seen a reflection of the monumental manner as practised by Sir Robert Smirke in London. He was the second son of John Foster, who held the office of architect and surveyor to the Liverpool Corporation, as well as that of engineer to the docks. He entered the office of James Wyatt, and probably acted as an assistant to Jeffrey Wyatt. In 1809 he accompanied the young student C. R. Cockerell abroad, and was concerned with that distinguished architect in the archæological researches at Ægina and Phigaleia. Returning in 1816, he entered into partnership in a building firm with his brother, from which he retired on the death of his father, to take up his father's work as surveyor to the Corporation. The Customs House and Revenue Building, erected in 1828 at an estimated cost of £200,000, is his chief work. It cannot be claimed for Foster that in the above structure he produced a work of superlative merit ; the composition of the plan is misshapen and unwieldy, and the general effect is incomparable in every respect with Gandon's building at Dublin. Notwithstanding these and other defects, the main elevation exhibits a fine sense of scale, which is well maintained. Foster was identified with the great town-planning improvements in Liverpool which took place between the years 1825–27, the designs for the street architecture of Lord Street and St. George's Crescent being prepared by him. Although he had not the inspiring genius of Thomas Hamilton or Cockerell, he nevertheless fought manfully for the development of the style in which he believed, and not without a meed of success.

The architectural improvements taking place in the great cities of the kingdom, not only in the individual buildings but in the comprehensive development of large areas, were likewise carried out on a grand scale in the city of Newcastle. In this connection the efforts of Richard Grainger were closely associated, although it is more than probable that he obtained assistance for the execution of his many schemes. He was originally apprenticed to a carpenter, and eventually worked with an architect. His mind was imbued with the idea of improving his native city, and after visiting London and seeing Regent Street he commenced operations on a vacant site of twelve acres in the centre of Newcastle, on which he erected in the short space of five years Grey Street, Grainger Street, and the market which was opened in 1835. He planned and erected, among others, Eldon Square, Higham Place, Leazes Crescent and Terrace, Clayton, Nelson, Hood, and Shakespeare Streets, the Royal Arcade, the branch Bank of England, and Lambton's Bank. Previous to Grainger's enterprise Neo-Classic architecture was but ill understood in the North of England. In 1812 the Courts of the County of Northumberland were erected in a version of Greek Doric by an architect named Stokoe, and in 1822 J. and B. Green designed the library of the Literary and Philosophical Society. It is certain that Grainger had the assistance of the former architects, as well as that of T. Oliver, and in all probability the advice and help of the talented Dobson.

Another important group of buildings representative of the Greek phase were the Athenæum and hotel at Derby, designed by Robert Wallace in 1837. He also erected the adjoining Derbyshire and Derby Bank, the latter an astylar treatment of great dignity enriched with refined ornamental detail.

THE GREEK SCHOOL IN SCOTLAND

The ascendancy of monumenal architecture was assured in Scotland ; in fact, more hospitable soil for its development could scarcely be found. The cities of Edinburgh and Glasgow, already noted for the number of Classic buildings erected during the previous century, were destined to witness greater triumphs of architectural skill. Nothing exceeded the enthusiasm of the group of Scotch architects who furthered the Greek phase until it reached its most cogent expression. The architects then practising interpreted the Hellenic themes with commendable austerity and reticence ; a distinctive manner resulted which was in main the outcome of a mastery of the laws of composition. One of the leaders of the new movement was Archibald Elliot (1763–1823). He started his career in London as a draughtsman to a cabinet-maker, afterwards returning to Edinburgh to practise as an architect. His sympathies were manifestly for the Greek phase of the Neo-Classic, although, like many other architects of his day, he occasionally lapsed into Gothic essays. From 1815 to 1819 he was engaged in continuing Princes Street to connect with Calton Street and form a direct approach from the London road. The completed scheme still remains one of the finest architectural features of Edinburgh. Elliot commenced this design by arranging balancing *motifs*, consisting of tetrastyle porticoes placed on basement storeys ; these form massive pylons on either side of the street, terminating a double group of buildings. The whole composition is linked at the centre by the screen to the Regent's Bridge. One of the buildings on the west side of the new

FIG. 85. WATERLOO PLACE, EDINBURGH, 1815–19   *Archibald Elliot, Architect*

FIG. 86. THE REGENT'S BRIDGE, EDINBURGH, 1815–19   *Archibald Elliot, Architect*

street was designed for use as the General Post Office by Joseph Kay, a pupil of S. P. Cockerell. Viewed from the lower street, the composition of the Regent's Bridge is very effective, and affords an impressive example of conventional scenery. In 1817 Elliot prepared a design for the Edinburgh County Hall, in which he introduced the Greek Doric order, but, yielding to inspiration after seeing the Elgin Marbles, he changed the theme in favour of the Ionic order from the Erechtheion. The arrangement of his earlier designs exhibits a leaning toward the style of Robert Reid and the brothers Adam. Notwithstanding this preference for the Edinburgh vernacular style, his buildings are an improvement on those of his predecessors. Among his pupils who carried on the tradition was George Bell, who entered into partnership with Clarke.

In Glasgow David Hamilton (1768 – 1843) occupied a prominent position as an architect. Between the years 1803–5 he designed Hutcheson's Hospital, in 1806 he built the Nelson Monument, and in the years 1829–30 the Royal Exchange, followed in 1841 by the buildings forming Exchange Square, with which he was assisted by his son-in-law, J. Smith. The Royal Exchange is rightly considered the finest Classic building in the city; it is distinguished for its dipteral octastyle portico, formed of lofty Greek Corinthian columns, and the graceful circular campanile. Notwithstanding the dignity which the main façade of the structure possesses, there is a lack of homogeneity between the front and side elevations, occasioned by the introduction of a pilaster order of different scale. The back elevation shows a resemblance to Sir John Soane's mannerism, more particularly in the employment of the incised lines used for decorative effect. In 1840 Hamilton designed the Western Club House, a building influenced by the Italian movement then apparent in London.

In the career of Thomas Hamilton, R.S.A. (1785–1858), is to be seen a broader rendering of the Hellenic theme. He practised chiefly in Edinburgh, and in 1825 he laid the first stone of the

Plate XXXI.

THE HIGH SCHOOL, EDINBURGH. DETAIL OF CENTRAL PORTION.

THOMAS HAMILTON, R.S.A. ARCHITECT. 1825-1829.

THE GREEK PHASE, 1820—1840

High School on Calton Hill; the building was completed in 1829. He erected the Burns Memorial near Ayr in 1820; and in 1830 he gratuitously supplied the design for the choragic monument to the poet which stands on the verge of Calton Hill.

If Hamilton's reputation as a monumental architect relied solely on his design for the High School, this building alone would secure his immortality. Apart from the fact that a study of the Thesion at Athens supplied the *motif* for this design, the paramount impression imparted to the beholder is the appropriate character of the building as a whole. The conditions of the site demanded a structure in which the horizontal line should predominate. Hamilton incorporated his design with the solid rock, and he disposed his principal and subordinate masses with skill and regard for the maximum effect of light and shade. His genius resulted in a building containing all the attributes of the monumental, and one, moreover, which in the history of English Neo-Classic architecture is of equal rank to St. George's Hall. Thomas Hamilton was not an archæologist, neither does he appear to

FIG. 87. THE ROYAL EXCHANGE, GLASGOW, 1829–30   *David Hamilton, Architect*

have travelled in Italy or Greece, yet he was more than conversant with the Greek architectural forms, which in his hands became pliant and docile. His design for the hall of the Royal College of Physicians in Queen Street, Edinburgh, erected in 1845, properly belongs to the Neo-Grec phase. Here again the principal factor in the design is simplicity, which, together with the harmonic distribution of the minor features and the importance of the focal point, reveals the handling of a master.

William Burn (1789–1870) was an Edinburgh architect of eminence who at the period divided the best work in Scotland with Playfair. After an elementary training in the office of his father he was sent to London in 1808 to enter the office of Sir Robert Smirke. On his return to Edinburgh he entered for the competition then started for the completion of the Edinburgh University buildings, being second to Playfair, and in 1816 designed his first monumental building, the Customs House at Greenock, which is an essay in Greek Doric. In the same year he erected the Merchant Maiden Hospital, using as a *motif* the Greek Ionic order from the small temple on the Ilyssus. The New Edinburgh Academy, built in 1820, was also a version of Greek Doric. In 1821–22 he erected the Melville Column, modelled after that of Trajan at Rome. The New

MONUMENTAL ARCHITECTURE

FIG. 88. BURNS MEMORIAL, EDINBURGH, 1830
Thomas Hamilton, R.S.A., Architect

John Watson Hospital, built in 1835, consisted of a principal façade composed of a hexastyle Greek Doric portico placed between two supporting masses; this is Burn's most important monumental work, and recalls the composition used by Sir Robert Smirke for the General Post Office, London. In 1844 Burn removed to London, leaving his practice in charge of his partner, David Bryce. In the capital his chief building is the mansion in Whitehall.

Probably no other Scotch architect had a greater reputation in the mind of the public as a monumental Classicist than had William Henry Playfair. He was born in London in 1789, the son of an architect of some repute in the metropolis. At the age of fifteen he returned to Edinburgh and attended the lectures at the Edinburgh University, eventually returning to London and studying architecture under James Wyatt and Robert Smirke.

He engaged in active practice at Edinburgh in 1815, and designed several of the terraces in the lower New Town, afterwards, in 1820 and the following years, designing the series of terraces, crescents, and streets forming the slopes of Calton Hill, including the Regent, Royal, and Calton Terraces, and on the north side of the city the Royal Circus.

In 1816 Playfair was successful in winning the competition for the completion of the University buildings, and carried out between the years 1817–24 the great Quadrangle as it now exists, as well as completing the design prepared by Robert Adam for the cupola. The Observatory on the Calton Hill he designed and erected between 1814–18; the Advocates' Library, 140 feet long by 42 by 28 (the exterior by Elliot); the monument near the Observatory, to his uncle, Professor Playfair, was erected in 1820. The Royal Institution, a version of Greek Doric, was designed by Playfair in 1822 and finished in 1836. With Professor C. R. Cockerell he commenced the National Monument on the Calton Hill, which was proposed to be similar in design to the Parthenon at Athens. St. Stephen's Church was built between the years 1826–28, the College of Surgeons and Museum, Greek Ionic, in 1830, Dugald Stewart's monument in 1831, and his last important work, the National Gallery, 1850–54, which he based on a study of the Greek Ionic order.

Like Thomas Hamilton, Playfair had no experience of foreign travel, yet both architects raised the architectonic standard of Edinburgh until that proud city received the appellation of " Modern Athens." Playfair was most thorough and fastidious in his taste, spending days and weeks over the *minutiæ* of his buildings; in this respect he resembled his friend Cockerell. The National Academy, on the Mound, is the finest

FIG. 89. SCOTTISH NATIONAL ACADEMY, EDINBURGH, 1850–54
William Henry Playfair, Architect

Plate XXXII.

THE NATIONAL GALLERY, EDINBURGH.
WILLIAM HENRY PLAYFAIR, ARCHITECT, 1850–54.

THE HIGH SCHOOL, EDINBURGH.
THOMAS HAMILTON, R.S.A., ARCHITECT.

Plate XXXIII.

THE ROYAL COLLEGE OF PHYSICIANS, QUEEN STREET, EDINBURGH.
THOMAS HAMILTON R.S.A. ARCHITECT. 1845.

Plate XXXIV.

THE TOWN HALL, LEITH.

MESSRS. R. AND J. DICKSON, ARCHITECTS, 1828.

Plate XXXV.

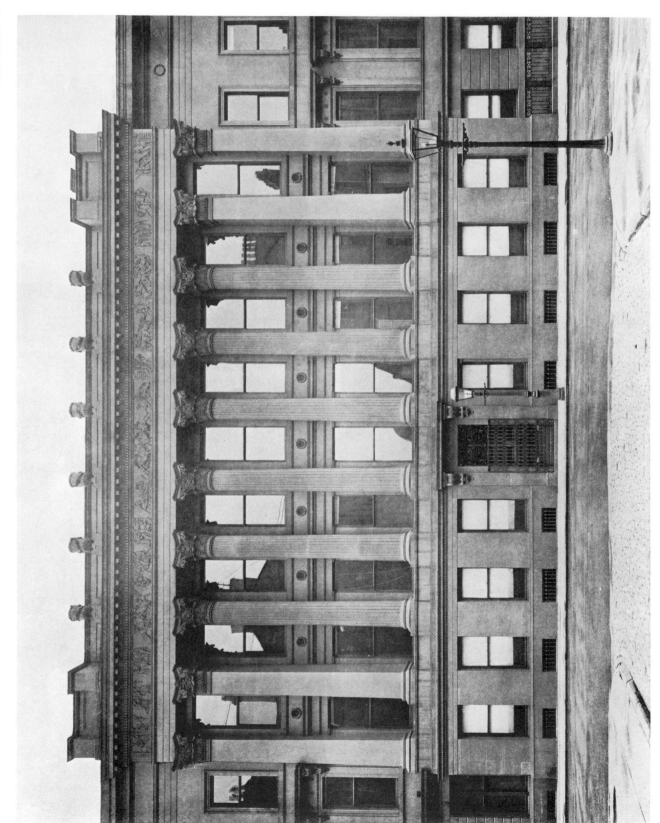

THE MUNICIPAL AND COUNTY BUILDINGS, GLASGOW.

MESSRS. CLARKE AND BELL, ARCHITECTS, 1844.

example of his exterior work, and the Advocates' Library represents the best of his interior designs. His monumental compositions are readily recognised by the simplicity of their massing, as well as by the strict regard for the academic use of the order. Playfair realised the necessity of introducing sub-*motifs* as foils to the comparative nakedness of the Greek style, and to this end he arranged his screen-walls, gateways, and piers supporting urns. A good example of his ingenuity in this connection is demonstrated by the screen-wall enclosing the Edin-burgh College of Surgeons. In this regard Playfair and Thomas Hamilton shared a common perception. His buildings never seem to lack warmth of feeling; this good quality was at-tained by the vigour of the selected ornament he apportioned to the parts that needed the most enrichment.

Playfair's design for St. Stephen's Church is very boldly conceived. No problem could be more difficult for an architect to solve than the design of a monumental church at the bottom of a hill. That he successfully accomplished

FIG. 90. THE MERCHANTS' HOUSE AND COURTS, GLASGOW, 1844
Clarke and Bell, Architects

this structure is a tribute to his painstaking genius, although one can hardly imagine why he introduced a pseudo-Gothic parapet to finish a Classic tower. He personally prepared the greater part of the working drawings for many of his structures, sometimes working on them for twelve hours a day. Unfortunately Playfair did not quite escape the fashion for Gothic then assailing Edinburgh, and his essays in that style were not happy. He closed his career at his house in Edinburgh in March 1857.

Messrs. Clarke and Bell were two Glasgow architects who actively advanced the academic style, their finest monumental work being the Municipal and County Buildings and Merchants' House, which they erected in 1844. This structure stands on an advantageously open site, the external grouping of the component masses is simple, and in the embellishments some of the Edinburgh mannerisms of Thomas Hamilton and Playfair are discernible. With the exception of the Surgical Hospital, built in 1861, which is of Greek character, their other buildings are mostly Italian in design. The latter include the Caledonian Insurance Offices, 1855, the Glasgow Barony Poor-house, 1859, the Water Company's office, 1860, and the city abattoirs. In Paisley they carried out the County Buildings.

The other notable Scotch architect who formed one of the talented group of Classicists was David Bryce; his work, however, will be described in the culminating phase.

The Greek phase of the monumental manner did not finish abruptly; the lessons taught by its exploitation received careful attention at the hands of the cultured men who at that time led the profession. After years of experience it came to be recognised that although the themes of antiquity were admirable in themselves, as forming the basis of the academic style, yet something more stimulating was necessary for the fostering of creative art. In consequence of the improved travelling facilities between England and the other countries of Europe, the leaders of architectural thought, of all nationalities, were brought into closer touch, and there occurred a simultaneous culmination of the Neo-Classic movement, which is best described as the Neo-Grec and Italian phase. Not only did the Classic school turn its attention with renewed energy to further labour in the fields of research, but it realised the value of broad methods of eclecticism, especially when the whole realm of Classic art in all its appearances could be drawn upon for inspiration. In the culminating phase is embodied the excellences of the style which preceded it, an acknowledgment of the great public works then in progress on the Continent, as well as a rare and discriminating perception of modern character. All architectural movements are found on analysis to run in cycles, each phase being productive of some masterpiece which excels in brilliancy of conception, the whole series belonging to its particular period. Such structures stand forth as the landmarks of style; they record the moods of the day which witnessed their erection; they add lustre to the ineffaceable seal of tradition, while enhancing its truths.

The evolution of a style is a matter for centuries; its stately progress does not recognise individuals, although their activities are essential to the slow growth, the blending of a series into one consecutive and indivisible whole. Architecture, to be truly spontaneous, must be conceived in that spirit of humility which, while desiring to expound new theories, reverently measures its opinions with the standard of past excellence.

In the succeeding chapters will be shown the extension of the monumental manner and the increased range of outlook engaged upon by Cockerell, Elmes, and Barry.

THE TAYLOR AND RANDOLPH BUILDING, OXFORD.   PANEL FROM THE ELEVATION TO ST. GILES

Professor C. R. Cockerell, R.A., Architect

Plate XXXVI.

ST. GEORGE'S HALL, LIVERPOOL. DETAIL OF PERISTYLE.

HARVEY LONSDALE ELMES, ARCHITECT. 1841. COMPLETED IN 1854.

CHAPTER V

THE CULMINATION IN THE NEO-GREC AND ITALIAN PHASE

PROFESSOR C. R. COCKERELL—GEORGE BASEVI—SIDNEY SMIRKE—THOMAS CUNDY—DAVID BRYCE—DAVID RHIND—HARVEY LONSDALE ELMES—JOHN GOLDICUTT—JOHN DOBSON— J. S. MULVANY—SANCTON WOOD—SIR CHARLES BARRY—PROFESSOR DONALDSON—THOMAS HOPPER—PHILIP HARDWICK—FREDERICK PEPYS COCKERELL—SIR WILLIAM TITE—SIR JAMES PENNETHORNE—CUTHBERT BRODRICK—EDWARD WALTERS—JOHN GIBSON—ALEXANDER THOMSON

THE incessant movement and progression attending the development of English Neo-Classic architecture found its most cogent expression at the middle of the nineteenth century, at a time when public opinion was singularly inappreciative of its academic qualities. The brilliancy of the style at its zenith was productive of great triumphs in modern design, a fact which gives cause for reflection, considering the counter-attractions presented by the experiments of the " Romantic " school. At this period Gothic was gaining the ascendancy in the eye of the public as being the only possible medium for architectural expression. Even the leaders of the Classic school are found pandering to the prevailing fashion in order to maintain their prestige. Yet, in spite of the absence of equilibrium, a series of monumental structures was evolved, with St. George's Hall at Liverpool as the climax. The lessons taught by the preceding Greek phase were blended with a free interpretation of Italian *motifs*, Barry's design for astylar buildings proving that columnar architecture was not always essential. The desire then expressed was to enter more thoroughly into the spirit of creative art which had fired the imagination of Phidias, Ictinus, and Praxiteles, to avoid the cumbersome machinery of archæology, which had served its purpose in forming the basis of the style, and to extend the experiences gained during the earlier stages of the movement. In these and many other laudable efforts, undertaken during a mechanical and commercial epoch, there is discernible something of the Homeric age, something eloquent of the idyllic Italian Renaissance, and, moreover, something essentially modern. The names of Professor Cockerell, Harvey Lonsdale Elmes, and Sir Charles Barry are pre-eminent among those who, while they demonstrated the suitability of the Hellenic *motif*, avoided the pedantic reproduction of its forms. They viewed the architectural problems of their day with the eyes of Greeks, full of appreciation for the purest sensuous beauty, never overstepping the limits of the academic, and thoroughly understanding the impartation of correct architectural character.

The virility of the movement has survived the indecisive attempts made during the past thirty years to resuscitate various styles more or less unsuited for their purpose. And through this connection, slender as it is, the Classical tradition linking the work of Inigo Jones to that of the present day is maintained. From the vantage-point of our own time we give heart-whole sympathy to the acknowledged achievements of architecture ; we applaud the works of such artists as Wren, Chambers, and Cockerell, we claim their thoughts and productions as our own, but we fail to understand that these masters employed the symbols in use in their day as a powerful aid to their architectural essays. Once this underlying factor is grasped, the segregation of principles from the complexity enveloping past historical styles offers definite possibilities. And it only remains for the conditions of to-day to be incorporated with the conventions of tradition.

Of absorbing interest is the life of Professor Charles Robert Cockerell, R.A. (1788–1863), who, apart from his archæological and architectural works, did so much to inspire a love of the fine arts. He was the second son of Samuel Pepys Cockerell, whose career has been previously described. After spending some time in his father's office he became confidential assistant in 1809 to Sir Robert

Smirke, and helped him in the rebuilding of Covent Garden Theatre until 1810. It was his father's wish that he should study abroad, and in April 1810 he sailed for Constantinople, which he reached after numerous adventures in December of that year. There he met three congenial spirits, Herr Linckh, Baron Haller, and Baron Stackelberg. Cockerell had already become acquainted with Foster, and the whole party was destined to become closely associated in many future explorations. The energies of the party in the fields of research resulted in the discovery of the Ægina Marbles and the Temple of Apollo at Bassæ. Cockerell travelled alone to Segeste and Girgenti, where he remained two months. During his stay at the latter place he attempted the reconstruction of the so-called Temple of the Giants, which was eventually published in volume form by the Dilettanti Society in 1861.

At the beginning of the year 1815 he extended his tour to Italy, travelling with Linckh as companion; they reached Rome in July of that year. Afterwards he journeyed alone to Florence, and spent some considerable time in that city, working both early and late, sketching and measuring the palaces. While at Florence his ability as a designer of sculpture enabled him to prepare a design showing the arrangement of the Niobe group in pedimental form, a composition which is now universally accepted. At this time he was asked to submit competitive designs for a palace to the Duke of Wellington, but experienced the greatest difficulty in making his ideas presentable. Disgusted at his failure, and in a moment of disappointment, he wrote and asked his father to let him give up architecture and become an artist. On the refusal of his request he renewed his studies and travelled continuously in Italy, eventually returning to Rome, where he completed his drawing of the Forum of Nerva. After visiting Paris in the spring of 1817, on which occasion he was much lionised, he reached London on June 17, after seven years' absence. There was something very fortunate about Cockerell's enforced stay in Italy; his renewed acquaintance with the masterpieces of the Renaissance gave him the hint as to the way in which he could adapt his Hellenic knowledge. His short stay in Paris during his journey home also enabled him to realise the necessity for modern architecture and the avoidance of pedantry. Long afterwards in one of his famous Academy lectures he said: "European travel, from St. Petersburg to Gibraltar, furnishes the most useful and practical source of education." Cockerell regarded the architect as the historian of his times, and never regretted advising his students to study the productions of their native land; he looked upon the orders of architecture as the letters of the alphabet, which awaited genius to cast them into discourses. He drew attention to the refinements of Greek architecture; speaking of the temples, he referred to them as being a kind of beautiful cabinet-work, enriched with sculptured jewels.

His immense knowledge of Classic art was drawn direct from the fountain-head of inspiration; he never descended to mere plagiarism, nor was he content with shirking the practical side of a problem, but always remained honest and truthful. He held in great respect the artistic triumphs of other contemporary architects, and was not above learning something from the achievements of his French and German contemporaries. Like Sir Christopher Wren, Cockerell began the practice of architecture somewhat late in life, although he had a far greater knowledge of form than had the former master. At the age of twenty-nine he brought from abroad a great reputation as a scholar which gained for him many friends and clients.

In 1818 he designed the Literary and Philosophical Institution at Bristol, which, with the exception of the circular portico, is an uninspiring design. No. 32 St. James's Square was built by his father, S. P. Cockerell, in 1820, and in all probability his son assisted him with the details. In 1823 an important commission was entrusted to his care, namely, the Hanover Chapel, in Regent Street, which was consecrated in 1825. In the planning of this building the architect based his design on the plan arrangement of St. Stephen's, Walbrook, while the composition of the exterior was inspired by the Church of S. Vincent and S. Paul at Paris, which Hittorff had recently completed. Previous to this he had made a design for a private chapel for Lord and Lady Middleton; the drawings, dated 1822, are now in the South Kensington collection. His original drawing for the Hanover Chapel exhibited an enriched pediment, a feature which would have materially enhanced the beauty of the erected structure. The imposing tetrastyle Ionic portico, which he based on the order from the Temple of Minerva at Priene, long afforded a prominent feature in the vista of Regent Street. Between the years 1829–33 he designed Trinity Church at Hotwells, near Bristol, and, associated with Playfair, he had commenced the Scottish National Monument on the Calton Hill at Edinburgh. In the latter instance the idea was to build a structure resembling the Athenian Parthenon; unfortunately, lack of funds prevented the completion of the scheme. In 1832 he built the Westminster Insurance Office in the Strand, recently demolished, and evolved the pedimental *motif* which he later devoloped and used for three of his important buildings. In the same year he was appointed architect to the Bank of England and designed the new Dividend Office in Threadneedle Street, which was removed in 1848 to make way for the present Public Drawing Office. As

FIG. 91. THE WESTMINSTER INSURANCE OFFICE, STRAND, 1832. DEMOLISHED IN 1908
Professor C. R. Cockerell, R.A., Architect

architect to the Bank he had great scope to exercise his genius. The design of the Drawing Office necessitated a remodelling of the attic storey on either side of the centre pavilion, forming the

south façade of the building. Cockerell replaced Soane's ineffective parapet wall with an attic storey of dignified design, recessed and connected with a balustrade. To-day the Threadneedle Street front of the Bank presents one of the most academic compositions in London, mainly as a result of Cockerell's improvements. In 1830 he entered into competition for the design of the University Library at Cambridge, but it was not until 1834 that fresh designs were asked for, and Cockerell's chosen. Even then only the northern side of the quadrangle was erected, partly owing to

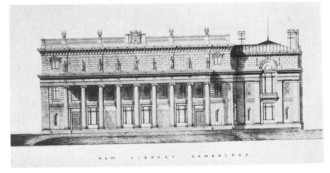

FIG. 92. THE UNIVERSITY LIBRARY, CAMBRIDGE
(Only a portion of this design is carried out)

77

the lack of funds, but mainly on account of a sentiment opposed to the destruction of the medieval buildings, which the realisation of his grandiose scheme in its entirety would have swept away. In 1837 he collaborated with Sir William Tite for the erection of the London and West-minster Bank in Lothbury. In this event the exterior was Cockerell's and the interior chiefly designed by Tite. The building as originally designed was not so lengthy as it is at present; but the drawings in the South Kensington collection show the front as it first appeared.

FIG. 93. THE UNIVERSITY LIBRARY, CAMBRIDGE. SIDE ELEVATION
Professor C. R. Cockerell, R.A., Architect

In 1839–40 he was applied to by the committee of the Sun Fire Office to design their new premises; the final design, practically as executed, obtained the unqualified approval of the committee in 1841. A careful study of Cockerell's preliminary drawings and sketch designs reveals the whole-hearted enthusiasm with which he always approached an architectural problem.

FIG. 94. THE SUN ASSURANCE OFFICE, THREADNEEDLE STREET, E.C., 1841   *Professor C. R. Cockerell, R.A., Architect*

Every line portrays a feeling for colour, every ornamental feature is selected with regard to its enriching the right portion of the building. His drawings are redolent with inspiration, and in this respect vie with his finished structures.

78

Plate XXXVII.

THE COUNCIL OFFICES, BRISTOL.

SIR ROBERT SMIRKE, R.A., ARCHITECT.

THE LONDON COUNTY AND WESTMINSTER BANK, LOTHBURY.

PROFESSOR C. R. COCKERELL, R.A., AND SIR WILLIAM TITE, ARCHITECTS, 1837.

Plate XXXVIII.

VIEW SHOWING PORTICO.

GENERAL VIEW.
THE TAYLOR & RANDOLPH BUILDINGS, OXFORD.
PROFESSOR C. R. COCKERELL, R.A. ARCHITECT. 1840-1845.

Plate XXXIX.

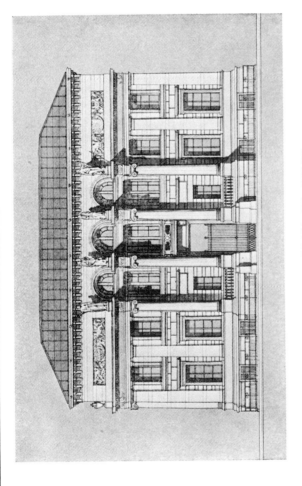

ELEVATION TO ST. GILES.

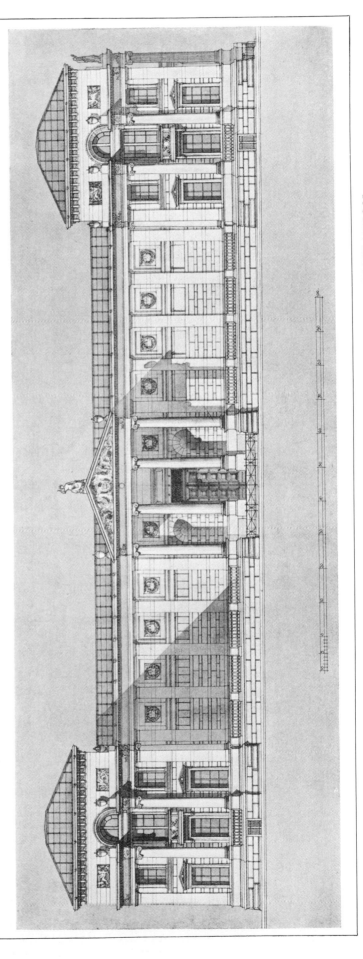

THE TAYLOR AND RANDOLPH BUILDINGS, OXFORD. MAIN ELEVATION.

PROFESSOR C. R. COCKERELL, R.A., ARCHITECT, 1840-45.

Plate XL.

DETAIL OF ELEVATION TO ST. GILES.
THE TAYLOR & RANDOLPH BUILDINGS, OXFORD.
PROFESSOR C. R. COCKERELL, R.A. ARCHITECT. 1840-1845.

Plate XLI.

· SCALE · OF · FEET ·

· DETAIL · OF · ELEVATION · TO · St · GILES · | · THE · ASHMOLEAN · AND · TAYLORIAN · INSTITVTE · OXFORD ·
PROFESSOR · C · R · COCKERELL · R.A · ARCHITECT
MEASVRED · AND · DRAWN · 1910 · E.Macman

Plate XLII.

THE BANK OF ENGLAND, BRISTOL.

THE BANK OF ENGLAND, MANCHESTER.

PROFESSOR C. R. COCKERELL, R.A., ARCHITECT, 1844.

Plate XLIII.

THE LIVERPOOL AND LONDON AND GLOBE OFFICES, LIVERPOOL.   MAIN ELEVATION.

PROFESSOR C. R. COCKERELL, R.A., AND FREDERICK PEPYS COCKERELL, ARCHITECTS.

Plate XLIV.

THE LIVERPOOL AND LONDON AND GLOBE OFFICES, LIVERPOOL. SIDE ELEVATION.

PROFESSOR C. R. COCKERELL, R.A., AND FREDERICK PEPYS COCKERELL, ARCHITECTS.

THE NEO-GREC AND ITALIAN PHASE

In spite of his wonderful knowledge of classic form he never arrived at the solution of a problem by hurrying. Almost nervously he felt his way, sketching out the suggested masses for the building, and giving point and prominence to certain parts as the design grew.

The Royal Exchange was completely destroyed by fire in 1838. After an interval of nearly four years, during which time a controversy raged over the merits of Cockerell's and Tite's respective designs, that of Sir William Tite was finally chosen, and the new works were commenced in 1842. Cockerell's design was in many respects superior to the building now standing, although at the time of the competition, as now, opinion on this point was widely divergent. From a monumental standpoint his design, had it been carried out, would have harmonised better with the Bank of England and the other surrounding buildings. He thought of the "Place" in front of the Exchange as the "Forum Londinium, and perhaps this is the chief reason why his design inherits features reminiscent of the Forum of Nerva. Cockerell used decorative pillars with their entablatures carried round them as vertical foils to horizontal lines; in this connection their use is eminently justifiable. He always thought of his buildings in relation to existing structures, and on many occasions went out of his way to design complementary architecture.

About the year 1844 he carried out the branches of the Bank of England at Plymouth, Manchester and Bristol, and in 1845 the stately branch at Liverpool. In 1844 he competed for the Carlton Club, in Pall Mall, but for some reason withdrew from the competition. In 1839 Cockerell won the competition for the Gallery at Oxford known as the Taylor and Randolph Buildings, the largest of his works, which he completed in 1845.

On the death of the talented George Basevi, who was architect for the Fitzwilliam Museum at Cambridge, Cockerell undertook the completion of that structure, the entrance hall and staircase as well as the library and fitments being detailed afresh by him. The charming staircase was subsequently mutilated by E. M. Barry, much to the detriment of the internal effect. At Kensington there is a beautiful design by Cockerell for the Wellington Monument, dated 1853, which was intended to have been placed in the Guildhall, but it was never carried out. The Liverpool and London and Globe buildings in Dale Street, Liverpool, were his last commission. In 1851, after the death of Elmes, Cockerell was appointed to continue the works at St. George's Hall, and from that date until their completion he gave of his best. The grandeur of the great hall, the dignity of the courts, the Dorian simplicity of the northern entrance hall, and the voluptuous elegance of the small circular concert-room are all the outcome of his painstaking zeal.

Cockerell took part in many of the important competitions of his day, and in at least half a dozen he was unsuccessful. Taking them in sequence, they were University College, Gower Street, the Duke of York's Column, the New Houses of Parliament, the Reform Club, the Royal Exchange, the Wellington Monument in the Guildhall, and the Carlton Club. Among his unexecuted designs were Falkland Palace, for Mr. Bruce, and sketches made at the desire of the Prince Consort for the projected South Kensington Museum.

As an archæologist Cockerell paid much attention to the restoration of ancient Classic work, and in many drawings gave conjectural ideas of the Roman Fora and the Thermæ of Caracalla, the Parthenon and city of Athens, the theatre and house at Pompeii, and the Mausoleum of Halicarnassus, a model and water-colour drawing of which, by Cockerell, are on exhibition at the British Museum. Abroad he had many honours conferred upon him. He was Chevalier of the Legion of Honour, a member of the Institute of France, of the Royal Academies of Belgium, Munich, Berne, Denmark, Genoa, Athens, of St. Luke's at Rome, and of the American Institute of Architects. When only thirty-one he was appointed surveyor to St. Paul's Cathedral, and at the age of forty-five succeeded Sir John Soane as architect to the Bank of England.

All Cockerell's later works were of such importance that it is difficult to give preference to any particular building as being his masterpiece. Opinion varies between the Bank of England at Liverpool and the Randolph and Taylor Buildings at Oxford. It is far safer to view all his creations from an impartial standpoint, as representing the finest solutions of given problems.

The great professor passed away in 1863, and was buried in St. Paul's Cathedral, which had been under his watchful care for forty years. His son Frederick Pepys Cockerell was left to carry on the

MONUMENTAL ARCHITECTURE

brilliant traditions of his father's works. Although at that time the Gothic flare appeared to outshine the Classic torch, in reality it was soon to be extinguished. The lessons taught by Professor Cockerell's buildings were quietly assimilated by men who at that time were unknown, and although the flame burnt low it is now awakening to greater refulgence.

George Basevi (1794–1845) became a pupil of Sir John Soane in 1811, and remained with him until 1816, when he left England for an extended tour through Italy and Greece. In 1819 he returned to England, and was able at once to enter upon the practice of his profession, being appointed surveyor to the Guardian Assurance Company upon its formation in 1821. His earliest works were two churches, St. Mary's at Greenwich and St. Thomas's at Stockport, both Græco-Roman in character. At the end of 1825 he was approached by Messrs. W. and G. Haldimand to prepare plans for the lay-out of Belgrave Square and the surrounding streets, and between the years 1825–40 he designed and superintended the erection of all the houses in that square, with the exception of those at the angles. The houses forming the centre features of the square are also the dominant masses of the composition comprising the sides of the square. In this important work of

FIG. 95. CONSERVATIVE CLUB, ST. JAMES'S STREET, W., 1843-45
Sidney Smirke and George Basevi, Architects

Basevi's is noticeable a blending of the style Neo-Grec with the Italian, especially in the masterly design of the ornamental features, such as the cartouches and supporting putti, which he placed in front of the attic storeys. His other town-planning achievements were Pelham Crescent, Sydney Place, part of Brompton Crescent, and Thurloe Square. The alterations to the Middlesex Hospital, including the remodelling of the main façade, were carried out by him in 1834; the latter is an effective monumental composition, with the pediment to the centre portions forming the climax to the vista from Berners Street. His masterpiece is the Fitzwilliam Museum at Cambridge, which best expresses his manner. With Sidney Smirke he was associated in the design and erection of the Conservative Club House, St. James's Street, the last important work on which he was engaged. The new club was commenced in 1843 and completed in 1845 on a site of what was formerly the Thatched House Tavern. The exterior of the building was the joint design of both architects, but of the interior decorations the ground floor was exclusively finished from Basevi's designs, and the first floor from those by Sidney Smirke.

In the spring of 1845 both architects were nominated to design the New Carlton Club in Pall Mall, but owing to Basevi's untimely death at Ely on October 16 of that year, whilst he was engaged in making a hasty inspection of the western bell-tower, Sidney Smirke alone carried out the building. In addition to the above-mentioned buildings, Basevi had an extensive domestic

Plate XLV.

THE FITZWILLIAM MUSEUM, CAMBRIDGE.

GEORGE BASEVI, ARCHITECT, 1845.

Plate XLVI.

THE FITZWILLIAM MUSEUM, CAMBRIDGE. DETAIL OF ENTRANCE HALL.
GEORGE BASEVI AND PROFESSOR C. R. COCKERELL, R.A. ARCHITECTS. 1845.

Plate XLVII.

THE BANK OF ENGLAND, LONDON. DETAIL OF CUPOLA.
SIR JOHN SOANE, ARCHITECT.

THE FITZWILLIAM MUSEUM, CAMBRIDGE. DETAIL OF CUPOLA.
PROFESSOR C. R. COCKERELL, R.A. ARCHITECT.

practice in all parts of the country.   His drawings for the Fitzwilliam Museum, Cambridge, together with those of Professor Cockerell, are preserved in the library of that institution.   At the Fitzwilliam Museum the portico is well placed to form the central feature between two pylonic masses, the whole

design being dominated by the square mass of the attic screening the stair-case domes.   Indiscriminate criticism has been noised abroad concerning this structure, mainly objecting to the plaster ceiling over the loggia, as well as to the apparent lack of cohesion between the front and the sides.   The grand scale and dignity of the main façade is above such petty interferences; sufficient it is that the author of the design gave Cambridge its finest Classic building.   The design of the great picture-gallery and the smaller galleries on the level of the first floor recall the method of lighting adopted for similar structures by Sir John Soane.   Basevi, however, never chanced into the strange mannerisms that marred Soane's later work, but preferred a straight-forward rendering of a Classic theme.   The design of the library, with the bookcases, fireplaces, and other fitments, is from the

FIG. 96. THE OXFORD AND CAMBRIDGE CLUB, PALL MALL
Sir R. Smirke, R.A., and Sidney Smirke, R.A., Architects

pencil of Cockerell.   Had Basevi lived to continue his architectural practice, England would have been the richer by many noble works; in practice, he was entirely in sympathy with Cockerell's ideas of eclecticism, and in thought thoroughly modern.

Although Sidney Smirke (1799–1877) never attained to the great reputation of his brother, Sir Robert Smirke, he was responsible for the design and erection of many meritorious buildings, which are representative of the later phases of the monumental development.   He commenced his career in the office of his brother, to whom he was articled, and whom he assisted until his retirement.   As a student of the Royal Academy Schools he was the recipient of the Gold Medal in 1819, and in 1820 commenced his foreign travels, visiting Italy, Rome, and Sicily.   In 1834 he remodelled the interior of the Pantheon in Oxford Street as a bazaar, retaining James Wyatt's north and east fronts; the present Roman Doric portico, replacing the earlier pedimented one, is by Smirke.   In the same year he designed the Custom House at Bristol, completed in 1836.   With his brother he designed the Oxford and Cambridge Club House in Pall Mall, which was erected between 1836–37. As previously mentioned, he was associated with Basevi between the years 1843–45 for the design

FIG. 97. SCREEN TO GROSVENOR HOUSE, PARK LANE, 1830
Thomas Cundy, Architect

and erection of the Conservative Club in St. James's Street. In 1842 he added the dome to the central portion of Bethlehem Hospital, which was originally built by J. Lewis, as well as the projecting parts of the east and west wings.

From 1847 until 1854 he was engaged on the enlarging and rebuilding of the Carlton Club, the *motif* for which he borrowed from Sansovino's Library of St. Mark at Venice. Although owing much to its prototype, this building does not present one of his happiest productions. His work at the British Museum extended over ten years, from 1847 to 1857, and includes the Roman and Assyrian Galleries, the Xanthian Room, and the iron railing and pylons in Great Russell Street. Acting on a suggestion made by Professor Hosking, he designed the circular Reading Room in the new central quadrangle. The Assembly Rooms, hotel, and Athenæum at Bury, in Lancashire, were built in 1846–47. The new galleries of the Royal Academy were designed by him between the years 1867–70, and on their completion he retired from practice.

Paradoxical as it may seem, his best work was the outcome of his collaboration with other architects. While he worked in double harness either with his brother, Sir Robert Smirke, George Basevi, or Decimus Burton his work was inspired, but alone and unaided he allowed it to sink to the level of soulless mediocrity, being content to resort to what amounted to plagiarism. His conception for the domed circular Reading Room at the British Museum is, particularly as regards

FIG. 98. SCREEN TO GROSVENOR HOUSE, PARK LANE. DETAIL OF GATES, 1830
Thomas Cundy, Architect

THE NEO-GREC AND ITALIAN PHASE

scale, the finest example of his unaided work, but the introduction of Lombardic tracery for the windows is quite unsympathetic with the Greek character of the older portions of the building. His great failing was indecision; he had neither the inspiration nor power for recasting historical Classic *motifs* into new forms. In consequence his buildings reflect a conflict of taste. Among his pupils were many who subsequently became eminent in their profession, such as Sancton Wood, G. H. Martineau, and Arthur Cates.

Thomas Cundy the younger (1790–1867) was the eldest son of Thomas Cundy, sometime clerk of works to S. P. Cockerell, and after the year 1821 surveyor to the Earl of Grosvenor's Westminster estates. He was associated with his father in many undertakings, and succeeded him as surveyor to the Earl of Grosvenor. This position he held for forty years, during which period he supervised the building speculations of Thomas Cubitt on the estate. Cundy was a highly accomplished architect, his most important monumental work being the Earl of Grosvenor's picture-gallery in Park Lane.

FIG. 99. GROSVENOR HOUSE, PARK LANE. THE PICTURE GALLERY   *Thomas Cundy, Architect*

He carried out extensive alterations to the London residence of the Duke of Westminster, and erected the fine Italian screen and gates fronting Grosvenor Street. Among many other important works in the West End he erected the Westminster Estate Office in Davies Street, and designed the grand staircase in Northumberland House.

The names of two Scotch architects must next be considered in connection with the culminating phase; their works represent a continuance of the traditions of the Scotch group described in the previous chapter.

David Bryce (1803–76), already mentioned, was the son of an Edinburgh builder. He received his education at the High School, and after a practical training from his father he entered the office of William Burn to study architecture, eventually becoming his partner. When Burn removed to London in 1844 Bryce succeed-

FIG. 100. THE BRITISH LINEN COMPANY'S BANK, ST. ANDREW'S SQUARE, EDINBURGH, 1850   *David Bryce, Architect*

MONUMENTAL ARCHITECTURE

ed to a very large practice.   His earliest work was the British Linen Company's Bank in St. Andrew's Square, Edinburgh, built in 1850.   This is an unusually ornate building, the effectiveness of which

is somewhat marred by the top-heavy character of the entablature which is carried round the isolated columns.   He practised chiefly in Edinburgh.   In 1853 he built the Adelphi Theatre, the Clydesdale Bank, the Subscription Library, and the North British Insurance Offices in Princes Street.   He devoted himself with all the enthusiasm of an artistic temperament and untiring energy to the practice of architecture, and attained to the foremost place in his profession in Scotland.

David Rhind, of Edinburgh, worked chiefly in a version of Italian, erecting in 1855–59 the premises for the Life Association of Scotland.   His

FIG. 101. THE COMMERCIAL BANK OF SCOTLAND, EDINBURGH

David Rhind, Architect

earlier building, the Commercial Bank of Scotland, erected in 1846, represents a Græco-Italian building of great refinement.   The sculpture on the pediment was modelled by Wyatt and executed by

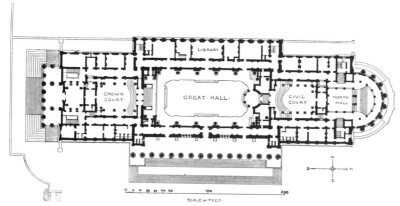

A. H. Ritchie.   The design of this building was inspired by the front of Playfair's Royal College of Surgeons, erected in 1830.   In this connection the Commercial Bank presents a striking instance of how one well-designed building will continue to exert its beneficial influence on the minds of sympathetic designers many years after its first novelty has passed.

Within the space of eight short years the career of Elmes had flashed with meteoric brilliancy across the architectural firmament, dazzling all by the intensity of its light, and on departure leaving tangible evidence of its transit.

FIG. 102. ST. GEORGE'S HALL, LIVERPOOL.   GROUND PLAN

Harvey Lonsdale Elmes, Architect

"Shall I send in a design for St. George's Hall?" asked young Elmes of Haydon, the sculptor. "By all means, my boy, and let it be something grand; none of your cut-up things."   Nobly Elmes obeyed the injunction, but how few of his predecessors did the same, and how many of his successors have done so since ?   Every phase of an architectural movement begets at least one really great monumental work.   Thus early in the history of the Neo-Classic development Sir Christopher

84

Plate XLVIII.

ST. GEORGE'S HALL, LIVERPOOL.

HARVEY LONSDALE ELMES, ARCHITECT.

Plate XLIX.

ST. GEORGE'S HALL, LIVERPOOL. DETAIL OF CIRCULAR END.
HARVEY LONSDALE ELMES, ARCHITECT.

Plate L.

ST. GEORGE'S HALL, LIVERPOOL.   GENERAL VIEW OF INTERIOR.

HARVEY LONSDALE ELMES AND PROFESSOR C. R. COCKERELL, R.A., ARCHITECTS.

Plate LI.

ST. GEORGE'S HALL, LIVERPOOL. DETAIL OF ENTRANCE DOOR.
HARVEY LONSDALE ELMES, AND PROFESSOR C. R. COCKERELL R.A. ARCHITECTS.

THE NEO-GREC AND ITALIAN PHASE

Wren evolved St. Paul's Cathedral, but a century and a quarter passed ere another structure of equal merit arose. Finally, coinciding with the culminating phase, there appeared at Liverpool St. George's Hall.

Elmes was born in 1814, the only son of James Elmes, an architect of considerable reputation in London, and an author of essays on artistic matters. After leaving school he studied under his father, and about the year 1835 entered the office of Mr. H. E. Goodridge, of Bath, as an assistant for three years. In 1839 particulars of the competition for St. George's Hall were advertised, and in July of that year out of eighty-six competitors Elmes obtained the first premium. There is a sketch of the original design, in which Elmes employed the Ionic order, preserved in the collection of the Royal Institute of British Architects. Being engaged to carry out the building, he sought to perfect himself for the work by studying the various domed works about London, and being attracted by reports of Schinkel's monumental buildings at Berlin and those of Leo Von Klenze at Munich, he extended his studies to Germany. In April 1840 he succeeded, out of seventy-five competitors, in obtaining the first premium for the new Assize Courts at Liverpool, and shortly afterwards received from the Corporation his appointment as architect. His design for this building, Greek Doric, indi-

FIG. 103. ST. GEORGE'S HALL, LIVERPOOL. BACK ELEVATION, SHOWING SCREEN
Harvey Lonsdale Elmes, Architect

cated the feature which is to-day so conspicuous in the composition of the present building, namely, the square-topped attic. After various meetings, and the submitting by him of several plans, he prepared another design showing the combination of St. George's Hall and the Assize Courts. This scheme was unanimously adopted, and on April 15, 1841, arrangements were completed for the erection of the united building.

In the preparation of the drawings Elmes was assisted by the staff of the City Surveyor, and he relied considerably for the superintendence and erection of the structure on the help of Mr. (afterwards Sir) Robert Rawlinson.

Although neither a scholar nor an archæologist of the calibre of Professor Cockerell, Elmes was nevertheless a man of keen discernment and thoroughly appreciative of the achievements of others. After his Continental visit and the occasion of his winning the Assize Courts competition he reconsidered his original ideas. Schinkel's first edition of "Sammlung Architectonische Entwurfe" appeared in 1840, and previously, in 1828, Blouet's monumental work on the " Baths of Caracalla " ; doubtless a study of these two volumes gave Elmes some idea as to the requirements of a grandiose plan. To a French architect the academic values a plan possesses are dearer by far than the treatment of elevations ; the simile also applies to the masterpiece of Elmes. The ultimate monumental character of St. George's Hall rested from the time of its inception on the horizontal trace of the vertical elements used in the composition. The plan in its directness and simplicity of grouping is masterly. True there are faults—what building is without them ? Yet, by comparison with other less inspired

85

plans, this one outshines them all. The plan of the interior is arranged on a central axis, the general idea being the vista, 300 feet long, from court to court, through the central hall. This idea of vista was of paramount importance in the mind of Elmes, and in reply to an enthusiastic letter from Rawlinson he describes how he intended it to appear : " When you contemplated the finished structure as it is to be, you stood on the judge's platform in one court, your eye glancing along the ranges of ruddy columns on either side in all the richness and strong colour of a foreground ; then reposing for a moment in the lofty arched opening communicating with the hall, whose broad and richly coffered soffit throws a shadow on the grey columns beneath and forms the middle distance, it pierces the atmosphere of the great hall, passes the corresponding opening into the other court, and finally rests upon the further judge's throne."

Judging from his numerous perspective sketches, Elmes had the ability to rapidly design a building in perspective ; not only did he prepare numerous sketches of the exterior, but also perspective views of the interior of the great loggia, and various other features. His full-size details, although Classic in spirit, are essentially modern in character ; every suite of mouldings received due consideration as to its placing, and its ultimate relation to the scheme as a whole. Nothing could surpass the beauty of the Neo-Grec ornament selected for terminating the dominating attic. The whole building fulfils the highest canons of the academic style, and is unsurpassed by any other modern building in Europe. In the spring of 1847 the architect's health completely broke down, his lungs were affected, and finally he was advised to travel to Jamaica. During his absence it was arranged that Rawlinson should superintend the work ; and before leaving England Elmes prepared drawings of all the outstanding items, including the decorative treatment of the great hall. However, he did not long survive, and died a month after his arrival at Jamaica in 1847, at the early age of thirty-three.

As previously described, the completion of the building was carried out by Professor Cockerell, the total cost amounting to £290,000. With regard to the design of the group of sculpture for the decoration of the south pediment, it must be remembered that Elmes applied to Cockerell for the use of this design long before the latter's connection with the completion of the works. Cockerell, after preparing the sketch design for the pediment, gladly availed himself of the advice and criticism of Alfred Stevens, who made certain minor alterations in the arrangement of the sculptured figures, and finally Stevens prepared a drawing of it for publication. Nicholl, the sculptor, who executed many of Cockerell's sculptural designs, was also responsible for the execution of this important work. After the death of Elmes an interval of four years passed before Cockerell was appointed architect; at this time the law courts, library, entrance halls, jury rooms, staircases, and corridors were finished, also the constructional portions of the ceilings of the great hall and small concert-room, and the external approaches had been partly laid out. In 1854 the whole structure was practically finished. St. George's Hall as it stands to-day epitomises the various attributes which constitute the monumental manner. Its site is magnificent, and the character of the structure stands for the dignity of official Liverpool. Apart from St. George's Hall, Elmes did not have many opportunities for practising in the academic style. His other buildings include the façade of the terrace nearly opposite Albert Gate, Hyde Park, and several mansions in the vicinity of Liverpool.

The history of the development of monumental architecture would be incomplete were a short account of the career of John Goldicutt (1793–1842) to be omitted. Although he had but few opportunities to execute great buildings, his sketch designs evidence such remarkable ability that the fact is all the more regrettable. Goldicutt entered the office of J. Hakewill as a pupil, and studied at the Royal Academy Schools. About 1814 he travelled to Paris and entered the school of A. Leclère, and sketched the ancient and modern buildings in that city. His studies eventually directed him to Italy, where he made measured drawings and coloured sketches for the works he subsequently published. Among the latter was the coloured drawing of the interior of St. Peter's at Rome, which is now at the Royal Institute of British Architects. In 1820 he returned to England and entered for the Post Office competition, in which he obtained the third premium. He also competed in 1828 for the New University buildings at Cambridge, and in 1830 for the Fishmongers' Hall, the latter a really magnificent design, in beauty of conception far exceeding the

Plate LII.

ST. GEORGE'S HALL, LIVERPOOL. DETAIL OF INTERIOR.
HARVEY LONSDALE ELMES, AND PROFESSOR C. R. COCKERELL R.A. ARCHITECTS.

Plate LIII.

ST. GEORGE'S HALL, LIVERPOOL.   VIEW OF INTERIOR, SHOWING ORGAN.

HARVEY LONSDALE ELMES AND PROFESSOR C. R. COCKERELL, R.A., ARCHITECTS.

Plate LIV.

ST. GEORGE'S HALL, LIVERPOOL. THE CIRCULAR CONCERT ROOM.

PROFESSOR C. R. COCKERELL. R.A. HARVEY LONSDALE ELMES. ARCHITECTS.

THE NEO-GREC AND ITALIAN PHASE

erected structure. In 1839 he competed for the Royal Exchange. His style showed great sympathy for the work of Cockerell, and he shared the same feelings as the professor regarding the transmutation of Classic detail. Nearly all his designs were drawn to an exceptionally small scale, the detail indicated with great accuracy and the colour scheme selected with confidence. His plans show a study of the principles of Durand. He published works dealing with Classic art, such as "Antiquities of Sicily," folio, London, 1819, "Specimens of Ancient Decorations from Pompeii," 1825; and in 1841 a pamphlet showing his design for the Nelson monument.

FIG. 104. THE CENTRAL STATION, NEWCASTLE, 1849. DETAIL OF APPENDAGE
John Dobson, Architect

The famous Newcastle architect, John Dobson (1787–1865), gave an impetus to Classic architecture in the North of England, the influence of which is apparent at the present day. At the age of fifteen he became a pupil of David Stephenson, then a leading Newcastle architect, after which period he studied in London under John Varley, the water-colourist. His stay in the Metropolis was his only experience of travel, but it was exceedingly fruitful because he became impressed by St. Paul's Cathedral and other more recent Classic buildings. His greatest achievement was the Central Station at Newcastle, completed in 1849, and opened by Queen Victoria and the Prince Consort. In this design Dobson's ingenuity was of assistance to the railway engineers, who acted on his suggestion for the curved platforms. A drawing of the station exhibited in Paris in 1855 gained him a *médaille d'honneur*. His monument is the city of Newcastle-on-Tyne, the greatest part of the public buildings and many of the finest streets of which were designed by him. Unfortunately, owing to expense, the City Corporation could not accept his designs in their entirety, otherwise Newcastle to-day would be the finest city in the kingdom. Dobson's characteristics were adaptability, patience, constructive imagination, and intelligence of the *genius loci*. With regard to the design of the Central Station, the effect the whole massing produces on the mind is one of simplicity, and, moreover, a simplicity which is maintained even to the design of the smallest details. Dobson approached this problem with directness, composing a great arcaded loggia as the central feature of an extended front, with balancing wings and terminal bays. He did not rely on the usual stock-in-trade of an architect for his effects, but from the outset subordinated all such elementary features to a simple composition of primary masses. Mention must also be made of the entrance gateway and lodges to Jesmond Cemetery, erected by Dobson in 1836, which is a monumental composition of superlative merit.

Ireland has produced many architects of renown, but few with the genius of J. S. Mulvany

87

MONUMENTAL ARCHITECTURE

(1813–70). Nurtured in the traditions of Gandon, and emanating from a family of artists, he started his career with every prospect of success. At an early age he became a pupil of William Deane Butler, and on the completion of his articles he was patronised by some of the first of the nobility and commercial gentlemen in Ireland. In consequence he became architect to the Dublin and Kingstown Railway and the Midland and Great Western Railway, to the city prisons, and several Dublin clubs, as well as architect of the asylum at Mullingar and a host of princely mansions.

As a monumental architect, such structures as the Broadstone terminus in Dublin, the terminus and hotel at Galway, and the station at Kingstown are noble specimens of his ability. He also erected the Royal Irish Yacht Club at Kingstown, the stations at Blackrock, Mullingar, and Athlone, and probably gave the architectural features for the great bridge over the Shannon. Mulvany's *forte* was the Neo-Grec phase of the development. Although he had a great admiration for Gandon's work, he never allowed himself to be unduly influenced by the ornamental tendencies of that master. Mulvany's father was Gandon's bosom friend, and afterwards his biographer, so there can be no doubt of his sympathies in that direction.

FIG. 105. THE BROADSTONE TERMINUS, DUBLIN, 1850   *J. S. Mulvany, Architect*

In 1841 he commenced the erection of the Broadstone Terminus on a commanding site near the King's Inns, finishing the main portion in 1850. The Ionic loggia for cabs and vehicular traffic was added in 1861. If any building expresses the character of its purpose it is this magnificent terminus, which so well illustrates the application of the monumental manner in a spirit of modernity.

Another architect who practised chiefly in Ireland was Sancton Wood (1814–1886), who early in life entered the office of Sir Robert Smirke as a pupil, and completed his term of five years with Sidney Smirke. His monumental buildings consist chiefly of railway termini and smaller stations. In 1845 he gained the first premium for the station at Blackburn, and in 1846 the first premium for that at Ipswich, and in connection with Mr. Bruff, C.E., designed many buildings for the Eastern Union Railway, including the fine " Italian " station at Cambridge which was erected in 1845. He became architect to the Great Southern and Western line in Ireland about this time, and erected the terminus at Kingsbridge. The station at Dumdrum was built in 1850, while the Cork terminus was designed by Sir John Benson.

The Kingsbridge terminus was his great work, and shows a laudable attempt to make a strictly utilitarian building architectural. The side elevation facing east, which is used for the departure side, is one of the best buildings of its kind in Ireland. Like Elmes, Mulvany, and Dobson, Sancton Wood avoided pedantry. In his completed structures he arranged the component masses with the utmost regard for monumental effect. Among many other buildings, he carried out in 1856–58 the fine range of houses comprising Leinster Square, Leinster Terrace, and Upper Hyde Park Gardens. In order to appreciate what the career of Sir Charles Barry (1795–1860) meant to the monumental movement it is necessary to limit the account to a description of his Classic buildings. After spending six years with Middleton and Bailey, to whom he was articled, he determined to study abroad, and, taking advantage of a small legacy left to him by his father, he started in 1817 on his foreign travels. He journeyed through France and Germany to Florence and Rome, afterwards visiting Naples, Pompeii, Corfu, and finally Athens. From the latter place he extended his tour to

THE NEO-GREC AND ITALIAN PHASE

Ægina, Smyrna, and Constantinople, and, meeting with a rich client, was persuaded to travel as his artist through Palestine to Egypt. Finally he returned to England by way of Rome in 1820, and in 1822 commenced what proved to be a great practice. Barry at that time did not escape the fashion for medieval architecture then in vogue. His essays in the Gothic manner, apart from those in which he was assisted by Pugin, prove him to have been as ambidexterous as most of his

FIG. 106. BRIDGEWATER HOUSE, CLEVELAND ROW, S.W., 1850   *Sir Charles Barry, R.A., Architect*

confrères. When in Egypt he was so impressed by the Temple of Denderah that from the day he first viewed that impressive structure he became a monumentalist, "henceforth to build with an idea and to build for ever." In 1821 he exhibited at the Royal Academy a view of the west front of the Parthenon. In 1824 he designed and erected his first monumental building, namely, the Royal Institute of Fine Arts at Manchester. This structure as regards the planning arrangements, external composition, and detail was at the time of its erection far in advance of any contemporary buildings, and was altogether a brilliant contribution to the Greek phase of the development. At Brighton he designed the Sussex County Hospital, also of Greek character, which was built in 1825.

The Travellers' Club, Pall Mall, erected in 1829 and completed in 1832, marked a new departure in Classic design, and besides being one of the earliest is undoubtedly the best of Barry's buildings.

FIG. 107. BRIDGEWATER HOUSE, CLEVELAND ROW, S.W., 1850
DETAIL OF ELEVATION TO ST. JAMES'S PARK
Sir Charles Barry, R.A., Architect

It is commonly supposed that the astylar treatment of the Travellers' Club and the Reform Club, both of which were designed in 1837, represented exact copies of the Pandolfini and Farnese palaces respectively; nothing could be wider of the architect's ideas. Barry, seeking for a *motif* by which to express the character of a club, selected the Italian Palazzo mode, and, assimilating the theme to his purpose, transmuted it by his own personality into an original design.

Between the years 1833–37, he carried out extensive alterations to the College of Surgeons in Lincoln's Inn, adding the "Cornicione" and unifying the façade. In 1850 he carried out additional alterations and built the magnificent stretch of panelled wall forming the rear façade of the structure in Portugal Street. Unfortunately additional alterations, continued after his death, have ruined this work. In 1836 he designed and erected the Athenæum Club at Manchester, and in 1840 carried out the foundations to Trafalgar Square and designed the parapets and steps. His next important monumental work was Pentonville Prison, built in 1841 (the magnificent entrance gateway has been demolished recently), designed after Haviland's radial system. The architectural aspect of this structure is grim and severe—in fact, almost as dramatic in character as "Old Newgate." In 1844 he carried out alterations to the Board of Trade offices in Whitehall previously designed by Sir John Soane, altering the façade considerably. Bridgewater House for Francis, Earl of Ellesmere, was erected in 1850; in connection with this handsome building, Barry prepared a fine scheme for the widening of Cleveland Row and the continuation of Pall Mall. It was intended to terminate the vista by re-erecting the Marble Arch between Stafford House and Bridgewater House, with a screen arcade on each side, similar to Burton's screen at Hyde Park Corner. In 1851, working in the same astylar treatment as he had recently used for Bridgewater House, he designed extensive alterations and additions at Cliefden, including the river-front; and in 1857 he prepared his great "Concentration" scheme for all the Government offices. Halifax Town

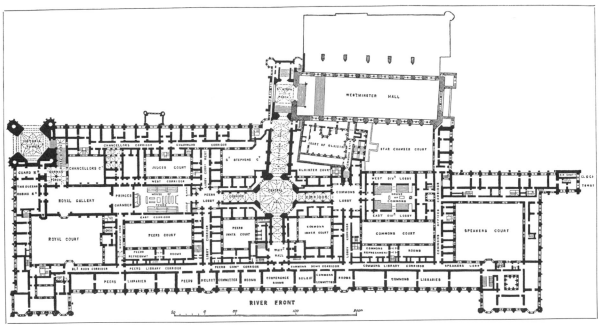

FIG. 108. WESTMINSTER PALACE, LONDON.   PLAN OF THE PRINCIPAL FLOOR   *Sir Charles Barry, R.A., Architect*

FIG. 109. THE REFORM CLUB, PALL MALL   *Sir Charles Barry, R.A., Architect*

MONUMENTAL ARCHITECTURE

Hall was his last work; it was commenced in 1860, previous to his death, and was completed by his son.

Although the Houses of Parliament are somewhat outside the scope of this volume, mention must be made of the building which occupied twenty years of Sir Charles Barry's life. In the first place the plan is a notable example of his Classic training, and in the second place the whole structure is conceived in a monumental spirit emancipated from the pettiness of style.

While his earlier works, such as the Manchester Art Gallery, the Travellers' Club, and the Reform Club are simple both in conception and handling, his later designs—such as the remodelling of Clumber Park, and the Town Hall at Halifax, are the reverse, being singularly devoid of restraint as well

FIG. 110. THE ATLAS FIRE OFFICE, CHEAPSIDE, 1838

Thomas Hopper, Architect

THE NEO-GREC AND ITALIAN PHASE

as complex in the disposition of the multitudinous minor elements. On the other hand, his plans were always academic in arrangement, no matter what style he worked in. His radial plan for Pentonville Prison, the grandly conceived plan for the Houses of Parliament, as well as his numerous town-planning projects for the improvement of London, prove him to have been a man of great ability.

The distinguished French architect Hittorff, when delivering an address at the Institut de France, on the life and works of Sir Charles Barry, said : " It was only after he had built the Travellers' and Reform Clubs that we recognised in him a capacity truly unusual, joined to a quality rare amongst the English, I mean a predominant sentiment of ' Art.' "

Barry at the height of his popularity led the Italian school, and had many followers and imitators ; his chief pupils were his two sons, Robert Banks, J. Somers Clark, and John Gibson.

As architect and author Professor Thomas Leverton Donaldson (1795–1885) greatly advanced the development of Neo-Classic architecture. He was the eldest son of James Donaldson, an architect and district surveyor of some repute. After receiving his education at St. Albans Grammar School he entered his father's office and studied at the Royal Academy Schools. In 1819, following the custom of the day, he started his foreign travels, which included Italy and Greece, and on his return published his researches at Bassæ in " Stuart's Athens." Beyond a town residence (now the Junior Athenæum Club) in Piccadilly, which he designed in collaboration with M. Dusillion, for Mr. H. T. Hope, the University Hall, Gordon Square, and the laboratory at University College, his works are limited. As Emeritus Professor at the University College he delivered a series of well-illustrated lectures dealing with the phases of Gothic and Classic art ; many of these drawings are still extant. His literary works include a collection of the most approved doorways from ancient and modern buildings in Greece, Pompeii and other parts of Italy, which were published in 1827.

The chief works of Thomas Hopper (1776–1856) reflect the Italian phase of the movement. They include Arthur's Club House, St. James's Street, built between 1826–27 ; the Legal and General Life Office, Fleet Street, 1838 ; and the Atlas Fire Office, Cheapside, built in 1838. The design of the last-named building is chiefly remarkable as showing what influence Barry's Italian mode had upon the return to the Roman and Venetian schools of the Italian Renaissance. Hopper's buildings are consistent in design and restrained in detail, and always distinguished by integrity of purpose.

The fame of Philip Hardwick in connection with the development of the monumental manner is upheld by several important buildings in London and Birmingham. Born in 1792, and trained in the office of his father, Thomas Hardwick, he inherited the latter's love of Classic architecture, which he amplified by tours in France and Italy. Returning to England in 1818, he began practice on his own account, and soon made a great reputation. After designing the dock-houses and warehouses for the St. Katherine Dock Company, which works he completed in 1825, he was appointed architect to the Goldsmiths' Company, and in 1836 he designed and erected the hall in Foster Lane. This design both externally and internally is at once magnificent and reposeful ; to the breadth of the Italian treatment is allied the finesse and purity of Greek detail.

When the London and Birmingham Railway entered the Metropolis, in 1836, Hardwick became the company's architect, and in this capacity he designed the portico and lodges in Euston Square, a gigantic version of the gateway to the Athenian Agora, the Ionic gateway and screen at Birmingham, and probably gave designs for the tunnel entrances at Primrose Hill. After 1838 he had the assistance of his son, P. C. Hardwick, who was associated with him in many of his subsequent works, including the great hall and booking-offices at Euston, the Victoria Hotel, the Great Western Hotel at Paddington, the Euston Hotel, the City Club, and the Globe Insurance Offices. The offices of the London and North-Western Railway Company in Seymour Street were also designed by the Hardwicks.

Dealing with the more important of his works, the vast hall at Euston, built in 1847, ranks as his masterpiece. The design is founded on Peruzzi's great chamber in the Massimi Palace.

MONUMENTAL ARCHITECTURE

The enterprise of the early railway companies in the sphere of architecture was remarkable, considering the immense amount of money lost during the time of the railway mania. The

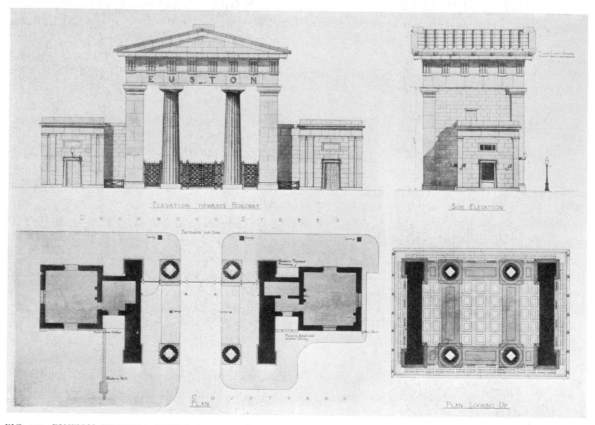

FIG. 111. EUSTON STATION, THE PORTICO

Philip Hardwick, Architect

directors supplemented the labours of their resident engineers by engaging the best architectural talent available to design the monumental works in contemplation, such fine structures resulting

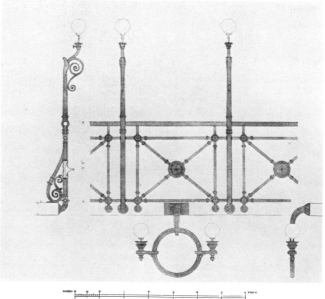

FIG. 112. THE GREAT HALL, EUSTON STATION. SECTION, 1847

FIG. 113. THE GREAT HALL, EUSTON STATION. DETAIL OF RAILINGS, ETC., 1847　　*Philip Hardwick, Architect*

Plate LV.

EUSTON STATION, LONDON. THE GREAT HALL.
PHILIP HARDWICK, ARCHITECT. 1840-1847.

FIG. 114. THE GREAT HALL, EUSTON STATION. DETAIL OF STAIRCASE, 1847   *Philip Hardwick, Architect*

as the joint station at Huddersfield by Stansby, and the pylons and other architectural features of the Menai Bridge by John Thomas of Birmingham.

Frederick Pepys Cockerell, born in 1833, was the second son of Professor C. R. Cockerell. He became a pupil of Philip Hardwick, whom he left in 1855 to continue his education on the Continent. After spending some years touring abroad, where he gained considerable experience of architecture and methods of design, he returned to England to assist his father. For the Liverpool and London and Globe Office at Liverpool he evolved much of the design.

These experiences exercised a ruling influence over his subsequent works, but notwithstanding he closely adhered to his father's manner. His practice was always good, but never very extensive, and mainly consisted of country mansions. In 1866 he commenced the Freemasons' Hall and Tavern in Great Queen Street, London. Not only does this building possess a conspicuous monumental character, but it represents a continuance of the

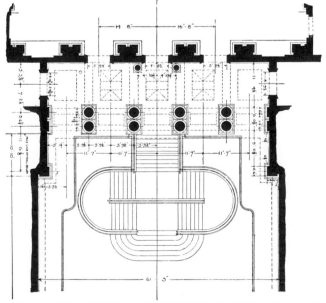

FIG. 115. THE GREAT HALL, EUSTON STATION. PLAN OF STAIRCASE

FIG. 116. HUDDERSFIELD STATION   *H. Stansby, Architect*

façade and interior alterations at the Pall Mall premises of the Society of Painters in Water-Colour. The beautiful memorial tablet in St. Paul's Cathedral to his father is also from his design.

FIG. 117. THE FREEMASONS' HALL, GREAT QUEEN STREET, LONDON, 1866
F. P. Cockerell, Architect

Professor's principles. The pedimental *motif* which distinguishes the three provincial branches of the Bank of England was modified and reintroduced as the centre feature of the new building. Unfortunately the obscurity of the site prevents this magnificent composition from being seen to full advantage. In 1870 he designed the Carlisle Memorial Column at Castle Howard, and another at Langley Park, in 1875 the

He was a personal friend of the eminent French exponents of the Neo-Grec style, Messrs. Louis Duc and Daumet, and enjoyed a high reputation on the Continent. Unfortunately, just at the time his career seemed most promising he died suddenly on November 4, 1878, while on a visit to Paris in his capacity as honorary secretary to the Royal Institute of British Architects.

The name of Sir William Tite is familiarly known in connection with the rebuilding of the Royal Exchange, a building which he won in open competition against four other celebrated architects. Born in 1789, he became a pupil of David Laing, and, after being unsuccessful in several competitions, he carried out, in 1832, the rebuilding of the Golden Cross Inn, West Strand, in connection with the prevalent "Metropolitan Improvements." His next important work

Plate LVI.

THE GOLDSMITHS' HALL, FOSTER LANE, LONDON.

PHILIP HARDWICK, R.A., ARCHITECT, 1829–1835.

Plate LVII.

THE ROYAL EXCHANGE, LONDON. ELEVATION OF WESTERN PORTICO.

SIR WILLIAM TITE, ARCHITECT.

was the London and West-minster Bank, Lothbury, which he erected in connection with Professor Cockerell, who designed the façade, while Tite was responsible for the interior. His other works include many of the early railway stations on the London and South-Western Railway, most of the stations on the line from Havre to Paris, and stations and termini on the Caledonian and Scottish Central Railways.

After the destruction by fire of the third Royal Exchange in 1838, the Gresham Committee took the first step towards the building of a new Exchange, and in 1839 a competition was instituted; this, however, proved abortive, and a further and limited competition was held between Sir Robert Smirke, Mr. Gwilt, Mr. Tite, Mr. Barry, and Professor Cockerell. Although Cockerell's design was much admired, Tite's was considered to be more imposing, and so the present building was erected, and completed in 1844 at a cost of £150,000.

The design of the Royal Exchange acted as a convincing argument in favour of blending the Italian *motif* with the Greek. Barry had previously fused the two styles with great ability in his design for the Travellers' Club;

FIG. 118. THE ROYAL EXCHANGE, LONDON. ENTRANCE GATES
Sir William Tite, Architect

and Professor Cockerell was one of the foremost to demonstrate how the whole experience of the past phases of Classic could be merged into a modern style.

The western façade of the Royal Exchange is commanding in character, and suggestive of the business centre of the city. The octastyle portico, formed of Corinthian columns, is an adaptation of that from the Pantheon at Rome, while the other portions of the building were inspired by the forms of the matured Italian Renaissance. The peculiarities of the site demanded a special plan treatment, and it is only fair to say that Tite handled the conditions in such a way as to evolve a magnificent plan.

Viewed in connection with the adjoining buildings,

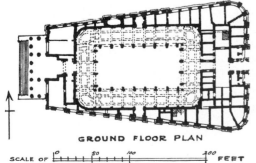

GROUND FLOOR PLAN

SCALE OF 0 50 100 200 FEET

FIG. 119. PLAN OF THE ROYAL EXCHANGE
Sir William Tite, Architect

97

FIG. 120. THE GEOLOGICAL MUSEUM, PICCADILLY, 1848

Sir James Pennethorne, Architect

the present structure is overpowering. This important fact was anticipated by Cockerell, who arranged his design to complement and to harmonise with the Bank of England. However, it is generally recognised that London possesses a Bourse which from an architectural standpoint is equally meritorious with those standing in Continental cities. Sir William Tite was president of the Royal Institute of British Architects between the years 1861–63, and again in 1867–70. He died in 1873.

The nineteenth century produced no architect more scholarly than Sir James Pennethorne, who, if he lacked ability for brilliant conceptions, deserves praise for the soundness of the principles he advocated. He was born in 1801, and at an early age entered the office of his uncle John Nash, who was then at the height of his fame. During the year 1824 he left England for an extended tour in France and Italy, and, returning in 1826, he again assisted Nash. After 1832 he was employed by the Commissioners of Woods and Forests to prepare plans for many improvements in the London streets. Among these were New Oxford Street, New Coventry Street, Endell Street, Buckingham Gate, &c.

He designed in 1836 Christ Church, Albany Street, and in 1837 Trinity Church, Gray's Inn Road, and the Bazaar in St. James's Street, which still stands. In 1837 it was decided to erect a Museum or Practical Geology, and

FIG. 121. THE GEOLOGICAL MUSEUM, PICCADILLY. INTERIOR

Plate · LVIII.

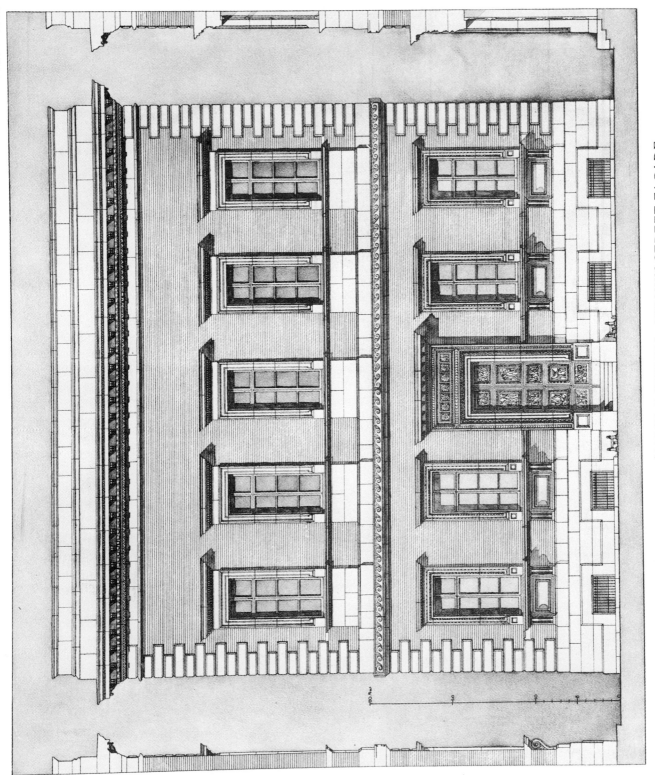

THE GEOLOGICAL MUSEUM, LONDON. JERMYN STREET FACADE.

SIR JAMES PENNETHORNE, ARCHITECT, 1838.

Pennethorne was commissioned to prepare the design; the completion of the present structure occupied eleven years. In 1848 he erected the new Stationery Office at Westminster, and in the same year removed the colonnade to the Quadrant in Regent Street and substituted the elegant projecting balcony in its place. In 1851 he designed the Ordnance Office in Pall Mall, and between the years 1852–56 he completed the west façade to Somerset House, which earned him the eulogies of his brother professionals. About this time a new ball-room was required at Buckingham Palace, and Pennethorne was entrusted with the work, which eventually included other additions. In 1854 he designed and erected the offices of the Duchy of Cornwall, followed by alterations to the interior of the National Gallery.

Pennethorne's masterpiece, the London University buildings in Burlington Gardens, was his last work in the Classic style. It was commenced in 1866 and completed in 1870, about a year before his death.*

Regarded as a monumental composition, this building is extremely fine. The sympathy of proportion between the centre feature and the appendages is well maintained, and the detail is of that exemplary type which always

FIG. 122. THE GEOLOGICAL MUSEUM, PICCADILLY. DESIGN FOR DOORS BY ALFRED STEVENS

characterised his work. No buildings could be more honest in design, and if the portico projects too far forward to harmonise with the upper portion it is a fault of little consequence. Vulgarity and bad taste were as foreign to Pennethorne as to Cockerell. He occasionally lapsed into megalithic heaviness, such as his two churches evidence, but these errors he more than atoned for by the elegance and refinement which distinguish his later works. Pennethorne knew the value of continuing a sound tradition, and while his works reveal his grasp of antique classic architecture their character is always unmistakably English. On the reorganisation of the Office of Works Pennethorne retired from service, and was knighted in 1870. His death occurred in 1871.

Cuthbert Brodrick was quite a young man when he succeeded in obtaining the first premium for the Leeds Town Hall. His subsequent buildings prove him to have been possessed of enterprise and confidence. With St. George's Hall, Liverpool, nearing completion it was natural for the young architect to turn to such a famous structure for his inspiration, and in some measure the internal character

* The original design was Gothic, and when changed for Classic the dominant vertical note in the elevation was retained.

FIG. 123. DUCHY OF CORNWALL OFFICE, BUCKINGHAM GATE, 1854
Sir James Pennethorne, Architect

FIG. 124. THE LONDON UNIVERSITY BUILDINGS, BURLINGTON GARDENS
Sir James Pennethorne, Architect

of the Leeds Town Hall reflects the interior of the Liverpool building. Externally the composition is effective and striking. The Corn Exchange, Leeds, is perhaps Brodrick's most successful work. The exterior suggests the Diamond Palace at Ferrara. His other important works include the Institute of Science at Leeds and the Royal Institution at Hull.

In connection with the development of the Italian phase the career of Edward Walters is of prominence. After some experience in the office of Lewis Vulliamy he visited Constantinople, and, returning to England in 1836, settled at Manchester. Besides many warehouses, offices, banks, and other structures, he erected between the years 1853–56 the Free Trade Hall, which is acknowledged to be the finest building in that city. The Manchester and Salford Bank in Mosley Street consists of an unique and rich group of buildings connected by an entrance of great scale. Walters believed in a rich simplicity for external architecture, and left his impress on the facial aspect of Manchester.

The influence of Sir Charles Barry's Classic style was long apparent in the buildings of his pupils and contemporaries. Among the best known of his followers was John Gibson, who was his pupil from 1835 to 1844. After winning in competition the new building projected in Glasgow for the National Bank of Scotland, he was employed for

Plate LIX.

Within drawing:

THE · DVCHY · OF · CORNWALL
OFFICE — LONDON

ELEVATION FACING S.t JAMES'S PARK

OFFICES OF THE DUCHY OF CORNWALL. DETAIL OF ANGLE.
SIR JAMES PENNETHORNE, ARCHITECT. 1854.

FIG. 125. THE TOWN HALL, LEEDS, 1858 *Cuthbert Brodrick, Architect*

FIG. 126. THE CORN EXCHANGE, LEEDS *Cuthbert Brodrick, Architect*

FIG. 128. THE TOWN HALL, LEEDS, INTERIOR, 1858

Cuthbert Brodrick, Architect

FIG. 127. THE FREE TRADE HALL, MANCHESTER, 1853–65

Edward Walters, Architect

Plate LX.

THE NATIONAL PROVINCIAL BANK OF ENGLAND, THREADNEEDLE STREET, LONDON.

JOHN GIBSON, ARCHITECT, 1863.

THE NEO-GREC AND ITALIAN PHASE

over forty years in erecting bank premises all over England. In 1862 he was appointed architect to the National Provincial Bank of England, and designed the head office and nearly all the important branches for that institution. In 1870 he carried out the Town Hall at Todmorden, and in 1878 Child's Bank, Temple Bar.

John Gibson gained courage by experience, and developed a broad and dignified Classic style, vigorous in the extreme and remarkable for the display of inventive faculty. It cannot be said for his works that they ever approached to those, either in composition or in charm of detail, designed by Professor Cockerell or Elmes. Notwithstanding, his buildings are distinguished for their virile character and general appropriateness. Gibson gave up practice about 1886, and died in 1892 at the advanced age of seventy-six.

No fact in the history of the classic tradition stands out in greater prominence than the career of Alexander Thomson (1817–75); but there exists a wide difference of character between his executed designs and the academic works of the other masters associated with the development. Thomson was a provincial in spirit, and owing to that was apt to exaggerate the value of the themes that inspired him. His mind was hurried away from the canons of the more orthodox phase of the Neo-Grec to attempt combinations of Hellenic and Egyptian *motifs*. He

FIG. 129. CHURCH OF ST. VINCENT, GLASGOW   *Alexander Thomson, Architect*

sought unaided to found a new architectural style, and in Glasgow succeeded in attracting considerable attention and not a few followers.

Although he had never enjoyed the advantages of foreign travel, he was enabled by the study of books to assimilate the finesse of Greek art. Doubtless his bent in this direction was given additional impetus owing to the influence and taste of Robert Foote, to whom Thomson was apprenticed. About the year 1849 he entered into partnership with his brother-in-law, J. Baird, and carried out works in Glasgow and the surrounding country. In 1856 he formed a partnership with his brother George. These connections were arranged by Thomson solely for the purpose of freeing himself from the business side of the profession, which enabled him to concentrate his attention on design. Apart from certain eccentricities of detail, mannerisms, and affectations, his buildings demonstrate tremendous courage and tenacity of purpose. He was the most enthusiastic designer of the nineteenth century, and by sheer genius succeeded at times in elevating his architectural manner to the level of the academic platform.

MONUMENTAL ARCHITECTURE

FIG. 130. GREAT WESTERN TERRACE, GLASGOW   *Alexander Thomson, Architect*

In the composition of primary masses was inherent Thomson's greatest power. Notwithstanding the difficulties under which he laboured, occasioned by the development of an individual manner, he handled the main and subordinate features of his buildings with purpose. His instinct for form was genuine, and although at times the buildings he designed exhibit crude contrasts between certain of the constituent features, the effect of the whole massing is always received at a single blow. Such fine structures as St. Vincent Street Church and the Caledonian Road Church in Glasgow are among the noblest of his works. During the closing years of his career he was occupied with designing blocks of terrace buildings in the residential district of Glasgow. Of these by far the most important is that in the Great Western Road. In the latter design is evidenced a greater suppression of individuality than generally characterises his work. The design of the whole composition is at once simple and effective ; two main masses are symmetrically placed near the extremities and slightly in advance of a lower range of terrace houses, with which they are connected. Nothing could be more simply conceived, yet by this procedure a far more satisfactory composition resulted than is evidenced by any one of Nash's Regent's Park compositions.

Thomson's predilection for abstract form in its enthralling mystery and dramatic intensity was the outcome of an original mind. His work in this respect stands alone, and while it reveals no sympathy for the broader and more academic rendering of the antique, as exemplified by the works of Professor Cockerell, Elmes, or Playfair, within its own sphere it is unique.

ST. GEORGE'S HALL, LIVERPOOL, SCULPTURE IN PEDIMENT   *Designed by Professor C. R. Cockerell, R.A.*

CHAPTER VI

CONCLUSION

THERE occurs a time in every man's experience when the limitations of his knowledge are suddenly widened, when a dazzling vision of brilliant possibilities arises, bringing with its aurora an awakening to a life of fresh inspiration and splendid endeavour. The genius of the soul is ever striving to extend the outlook of human intelligence, to fathom the truths of nature which in their forceful simplicity prove so elusive, to bring into clearer vision the laws of breadth, universality, blitheness, and repose, and to dower mankind with the spirit of the Eternal. All through the ages this restlessness has been characteristic of the tireless energy of man, who, seldom content with one settled mode of expression, has endeavoured, not without success, to emulate the grandeur which immerses our lives.

Architecture and the kindred arts are the outcome of this appeal to the intellect : their development presents the varied emotions experienced, while interpenetrating and permeating the objects themselves there is an underlying sense of remoteness, in itself a part of nature. It is in the detachment and sequestration of one object from another, in the pursuit of one definite trend of thought rather than a preference for many, that the finer distinctions of style inhere. Thus the great periods in art form self-contained circles, each reacting the one on the other, each within its own circumference enclosing the rise, the culmination, and the decline of a certain phase of art, each showing an indelible record of the manners, customs, and style of a people. Examine any particular period of art, and style will be found there ; the conditions of the time have shaped the whole and left their impress thoroughly and faithfully, and in such manner as no other temper or other age could have produced.

Although this is true in some degree of all the phases of art, it is most apparent in those tremendous periods when the world was yet young ; at a time when the monumental architecture and sculpture of Egypt and Assyria were being quickened into vigorous life by Hellenic fire. During the Periclean age, an age rich in intellect, great, true, and free in temper, an age which produced Ictinus and Phidias in one group and Plato, Socrates, Thucydides, Euripides and Æschylus in another, the art of the antique world reached its zenith. With the fusion of Dorian and Ionian art at Athens, during the fifth century B.C., there ensued a wonderful climax, the like of which the world can never experience again. In the evanescent period of the Athenian culmination it appears as though the thoughts and ambitions of antiquity were crystallising for all time, were formed into one pæan of praise, the swan song of an ideal and natural world. Even the decline was productive of works of rare beauty. The Hellenic temperament died slowly. Like rose-petals strewn by a storm the works of art were torn from their native setting to adorn the halls of the conquerors. The Romans, with all their vaunted glory, could not escape the spell of Hellas. They partook of its fragrance long before their materialism impelled them to paths of conquest, and they interpreted its meaning to accord with their own view of life. After Rome came the long night when Classic art slept, to be followed by the glorious dawn of the Italian Renaissance, the reawakening to a life of positive results.

The history of the true Renaissance begins and ends in Italy : it was a complete movement within itself, owing little to outside influences. Possibly the last breath of the dying Eastern Empire of Byzantium fanned into leaping flame the smouldering embers of Classic thought ; and, on the other hand, the peoples of Italy were not attracted to the cold mysticism of Gothic art : they inherited the Greek spirit—they were still in sympathy with the humanism of Greece and Rome. Northward, through the agency of the Renaissance, the spirit of Hellenism reached France and England, and at a later date Germany. The artists of Italy were the first to demonstrate to the rest of the world the forceful refinement of the old culture : they evolved distinctive schools of architecture, painting, and sculpture ; they revived literature and unconsciously directed the attention of posterity to unsuspected truths.

MONUMENTAL ARCHITECTURE

Passing to a study of English architecture we reach the first quarter of the seventeenth century, when the Classic spirit had obtained a sure hold on the imagination of Englishmen. This period was an adventurous one, and, moreover, one peculiarly suited to the furtherance of new and encouraging thought. The literature of that day not only reflected the voyagings and discoveries of Englishmen in all parts of the world, but it presented a curious admixture of paganism interwoven with native lore. In a great measure the architecture reflected a similar tendency until the opportune moment arrived when the genius of Inigo Jones gave a definite tangibility to what had hitherto been a drifting movement. In the Devonshire collection of drawings at Chatsworth there are several designs by this master for the new buildings at Whitehall, which, considering the date of their conception, are remarkable for the monumental qualities suggested.

We can imagine the difficulties besetting the path of an architect at this juncture, the lack of trained workmen to execute the finest detail, the necessity to superintend every item personally ; then, on the other hand, as if to balance the difficulty, there were the king and his courtiers eagerly extending their patronage to the arts. Monumental and refined as the design of the Banqueting Hall is, considering the early date of its erection, it is but the forerunner of a series of other and nobler structures, the building of which extends from the early seventeenth century practically to within our own time. Breadth, centrality, and repose are the hall-marks of English monumental architecture, *motifs* culled with honesty of purpose from the ruins of antiquity. In the buildings associated with the name of Sir Christopher Wren there is apparent the same underlying sense of the monumental, a similar striving for the noblest form of expression. He could not emancipate himself from the loose ornamental tendencies of the period in which he laboured ; but the freedom and licence of the contemporary ornamentation were almost entirely negatived by the masterly sense of massing and proportion which even his smallest buildings show.

The age of Wren was succeeded by the age of scholarship ; men inquired more thoroughly into the moving spirit of Hellas, the age of good sense ensued, which even the disturbing element of the French *rocaille* failed to upset. The cult of monumental architecture, in its more academic phase, is coincidental with the influence of the coterie of amateurs led by that fashionable dilettante Lord Burlington. We can afford to pass over the minor works of the first half of the eighteenth century, such as the country mansions of the nobility, and certain structures which do not come within the meaning of the term academic, to concentrate our attention on those of supreme importance. In the works of Sir William Chambers and James Gandon there is to be seen a fuller acceptance of the antique spirit ; these talented men were endeavouring to interpret the composition and monumental character of the works of old Rome. Their buildings cannot in any sense be held to be copies of antique prototypes ; they are original compositions, owing nothing more than the permeating spirit to the style which inspired their design. Contrary to expectation, with each new discovery in the fields of research, each new exhumation and bringing to the surface of some masterpiece of Hellenic art, the even tenour of English Classic architecture proceeded with almost imperceptible change. To the vernacular rendering of a Classic style, now firmly established, the purity and finesse of Greek detail lent an added charm and *naïveté*, a freshness and vivacity of expression.

The publication of the researches undertaken by Stuart and Revett in Greece gave a new impetus to the arts in Europe, and prepared the way for the rigid architectural discipline of the early years of the nineteenth century. The *furore* for Greek art, manifested at this period in fashionable circles, was met by some architects in a very broad and not unreasonable manner, the work of the brothers Adam being a case in particular, their designs reflecting an imaginative handling of Greek detail, not very vigorous, but redolent with delicate and charming feeling. About this period the evolution of English Classic architecture branched into two separate channels, each bearing a distinct relation the one to the other, but separated by differences of handling. Hence the work of the brothers Adam, James Wyatt, Joseph Bonomi, and other contemporary architects of less renown show tendencies essentially ornamental, while the monumental manner was more fully expounded by Chambers, Gandon, Holland, and Dance. With the close of the eighteenth century the stronger phase alone survived, carrying with impetus, well into the nineteenth, the charms of the old grand style to blend

CONCLUSION

with modern thought. Of this transitional period much could be written—sufficient to say it produced Soane, Nash, and Smirke, it witnessed the importation of the Elgin Marbles, and it finally saw public opinion focussed on Greece. Viewed in retrospective, the buildings of this experimental age, although monumental in aspect and chaste in design, lack the element of warmth which is among the attributes of fine art. The exponents of the Greek phase were so enamoured of and carried away by the austerity of pure Greek architecture that in some instances they neglected to endow their creations with depth of feeling ; they felt that the purity of the Hellenic *motifs* was all-sufficient and that anything they might add would only be attempting to paint the lily. In this regard the logic exercised was unsound and led the school into unimportant side issues, the result of undue archæological tendencies. Not the least responsible factor which militated against the arts was the wars then devastating Europe, causing the limitation of travel and cosmopolitan intercourse, and the general distress. With the universal peace which followed Waterloo the arts in Europe again prospered ; Germany and other nations entered the archæological arena, vying with England in promoting a knowledge of the antique. The architecture of the Greek phase, in its lack of warmth and enterprise, was only a reflex of the stagnation of creative impulse caused by the dramatic career of the Napoleonic legions, yet this halting period evolved sound eclectic views and heralded the Neo-Grec culmination.

If reference is made to the literature of the day, and more especially to the essays of those in a position to influence public taste, the elevation of the Greek theme stands clear above all others. The " Ode on a Grecian Urn," written by Keats, fitly explains the general estimation and attitude towards objects of art :

> Thou still unravished bride of quietness,
> Thou foster-child of silence and slow time,
> Sylvan historian, who canst thus express
> A flowery tale more sweetly than our rhyme :
> What leaf-fringed legend haunts about thy shape
> Of deities or mortals or of both,
> In Tempe or the dales of Arcady ?
> What men or gods are these ? What maidens loth ?
> What mad pursuit ? What struggles to escape ?
> What pipes and timbrels ? What wild ecstasy ?

The nineteenth century proved to be an age in which the idealistic tendency in all spheres of art gained the ascendancy ; but strong as the catholicity of taste became it could not overthrow the deeply rooted regard for the academic features of pure Classicism.

The tentative experiments of the Greek phase were reinforced by an extension of the artistic horizon to include all phases of Classic art ; Greek finesse was studied and appreciated in proper perspective, artists were no longer content to reproduce obvious Classic features. They still resorted to the themes of antiquity for inspiration, but the day had long since passed when nature could be studied other than through the conventions of the ages. Truthful and original compositions expressive of and demonstrating their mission were striven for ; and that evasive and subtle quality, rightness of character, was imparted to architectural designs. Herein lies one of the greatest of the many difficulties which beset modern architects, the supreme and imaginative handling of material to express concrete character. Practical architecture can only show by indeterminate hints or by vague symbol the opinion and purpose intended by the architect. If he be a scholar he is careful to consider the little facts which ensure his building being conceived in a grammatical key. Should he be a stylist he faithfully follows the tenets of the phase of art in which he is working, but the successful impartation of character implies more than the foregoing ; in brief, it means suitability of conception.

The Neo-Grec and Italian culmination provided a fitting climax to a sustained movement, which had been in existence for nearly three hundred years. Undeterred by the attractions of the Gothic school, the leaders of thought succeeded in harmonising fastidious Classic taste with the exigencies of modern life. To appreciate the English culmination in its widest sense it is necessary to take into consideration the achievements of foreign architects, so that some idea of the cosmopolitan character of the style can be grasped. The influence of the English researches in Greece and Asia Minor had its first fruits among the architects of France and Germany during the first quarter of the last century. In the former country Hittorff erected the church of St. Vincent and St. Paul at Paris, and at a later date he carried out the magnificent façade to the Gare du Nord. The remodelling by Louis Duc of the Palais de Justice, the building of the exquisite library of St. Genéviève by Labrouste, and the elegant library of the École des Beaux-Arts by Duban are all structures distinguished by their purity of conception. In Germany Carl Friedrich Schinkel was responsible for the design of the most important monumental buildings which enrich modern Berlin. Such were the activities of the age a few years after Professor Cockerell returned from his lengthy tour in Greece and Italy. About the year 1820 the English influence on American Governmental buildings began to assert itself, and it continued until the year 1850. This period was followed in America by one of artistic stagnation, but the Classic tradition had had sufficient time to take root, and to-day it forms the mainstay of American architecture.

FIG. 131. OLD SAVINGS BANK, QUEEN VICTORIA STREET, LONDON   *John Williams, Architect*

While all this intense pursuit of the ideal was taking place abroad there were architects and artists in England whose talent was world-famous. To the names of Cockerell and Barry must be added that of Elmes, the brilliant and youthful genius whose life flickered out at the hour of his success. In the magnificent fecundity of Professor Cockerell's designs and executed works is reflected the English version of Neo-Grec architecture. His fresh interpretation of the Classic spirit, the deep respect and regard for tradition, and the intensity of the imaginative reasoning depicted in his buildings, make sweet appeal to the intellect. Both Cockerell and Elmes were not above learning from their brilliant German contemporary Schinkel, but whatever they borrowed they made entirely their own. The employment of the astylar *motif*, in likeness of the Italian palace, by Sir Charles Barry gave further and more piquant interest to the movement until Alexander Thomson attempted his individual style at Glasgow. The highest notes in the gamut of the monumental manner were struck by the erection of public buildings of the first rank ; yet the search for architectural perfection extended even to the design of structures whose purpose was primarily utilitarian. Feats of architectural engineering were accomplished in the style, and the elasticity and sanity of the Classic *motif* was proved.

The culminating phase of monumental architecture extended to practically as recent a date as 1870 ; in truth it exists later in the form of a wonderful aftermath, a further growth, the products of which connect the main movement to the events which are taking place to-day. The school of design engendered by the leadership of Professor Cockerell inspired the evolution of such monumental structures as the series of post-offices designed for the Office of Works by their architect, James Williams. In this regard the building at the junction of St. Martin's-le-Grand with Newgate Street, the Old Savings Bank in Queen Victoria Street, and the splendid pile at Manchester deserve the highest consideration. The other buildings conceived in the grand style comprise the School of Medicine in Giltspur Street, by Edward I'Anson, and the eastern extension to the British Museum, which was completed in 1883. The Harris Library at Preston, built between the years

CONCLUSION

1883–96 by James Hibbert, is perhaps the most recent building erected in England which follows the academic tradition. Its design and character are strikingly appropriate; it embodies the lessons of the English manner combined with the Neo-Grec detail of Louis Duc and Labrouste.

Underlying our modern culture there still exists the spirit of Hellenism—that fire of ancient art which, paradoxical as it may seem, is the essence of all sound design. The universal language spoken by the architecture of Greece, Rome, and Italy is the compelling force which charms the intellect—the message it brings is one of humanity, purity, and refinement. In the stress and excitement of modern life, with its complexity, its distractions, and diverse interests, how difficult it has become for us to forsake the snare of passing fashion in art to return to the completeness of the definite Hellenic style! The noblest form of architecture, the monumental, demands this oneness, this intellectual and academic centrality. This is what the furtherance of the Classic spirit implies; the working of the imaginative intellect on the tried masterpieces of art, and this is the only method which can assure legitimate originality. When we visit a gallery of sculpture or a museum containing varied collections we are confused by the vast array of perplexing objects: how true this simile is becomes clear when we apply it to the great number of past historical styles; we stand amazed at their interpenetration, at the numerous side issues and departures from the orthodox trend. This is the position of the majority of architects and the public audience at the present time: an uncertainty, an unbounded amazement, an indecision which is more than regrettable.

The language of architecture is composed of three main principles, which must always be borne in mind if true art is desired; these are: the habit of assimilation, the gift of delineation, and the power of expression in the concrete. Real architecture never consists of a voiceless arrangement of lines, ornaments, and features selected at random; it always appears as the lasting representation of a definite and intellectual idea.

Although it is argued that the scientific attitude of the present age, with its exact

FIG. 132. THE GENERAL POST OFFICE, NEWGATE STREET, LONDON   *James Williams, Architect*

FIG. 133. THE SCHOOL OF MEDICINE, ST. BARTHOLOMEW'S, LONDON   *Edward L'Anson, Architect*

109

MONUMENTAL ARCHITECTURE

modern rules and formulæ, is opposed to the development of a national style; we have only to review the great strides made of recent years in America to understand the advantages of an academic school. It is this modern rendering of the antique style, which lends such charm and interest to the monumental works of McKim, Mead, and White; their work is great because it has assimilated something of the greatness which hovers over those ancient buildings constituting the standard of taste for the world. America is slowly but surely creating unto herself a distinct style; and one, moreover, which is excellent in architectural values, because it embraces the theory of the Classic spirit without being a return to mere mechanical pedantry. In spite of the importation of the style of the Beaux-Arts, with its concomitant attempts to Parisianise American architecture,

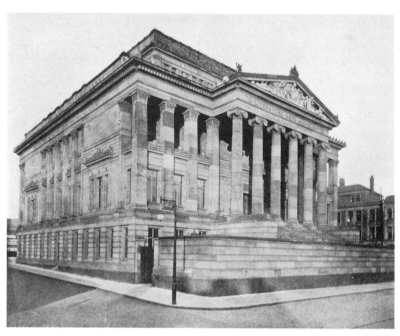

FIG. 134. THE HARRIS LIBRARY, PRESTON, 1883-96   *James Hibbert, Architect*

the Anglo-Saxon reticence has maintained its authority. Do we not see in this activity the sound influence of the English school—an influence which communicated itself to American architecture at a time when that country was young and impressionable? Even as the Dorian colonists, in Sicily, evolved a distinctive style which in time blended with and reacted on the Ionian element at Athens; so history repeats itself, and the modern Classic movement in America is already a powerful agency and spur to the arts of Europe. The art and practice of architecture is esoteric, it can never be rightly understood by the majority of the public, who only receive their impressions in a vague kind of way. When architecture becomes popular and fashionable it loses its higher qualities, it makes no especial appeal to the intellect, it merely quickens the imagination to a sense of the gay and trivial. But there exists no reason why the finest architecture should not become popular in an intellectual sense, and by its uplifting character improve the culture of the race. Monumental architecture radiates

FIG. 135. THE HARRIS LIBRARY, PRESTON, THE ROTUNDA
James Hibbert, Architect

character and inspiration, it clothes with the mantle of dignity all who frequent its precincts.

The particular, especially in England, in which the modern interpretation of Classic architecture

CONCLUSION

fails is the neglect of simplicity in the composition of the primary masses of a building. Reasoning is the basic principle of design. All the masterpieces of architecture portray the logical thinking out and apportioning of the features which form the constituent elements of their mass. Yet simplicity is not the effect attempted in the majority of English buildings ; its place is usurped by an assertive originality, a mere, and oftentimes unconscious, caricaturing of the academic quality. Refinement in the detail of mouldings, undue richness in ornamentation and redundancy of features do not accomplish ideal building. Chastity in architectural design is only procured by the exercise of restraint as well as conformity to laws planted deep in the womb of things. In monumental design formalism and mass are of paramount importance, rhythm and completeness are next in order, while the maintenance of scale in every minor element, with austerity and refinement, is an essential attribute.

From the time when Inigo Jones erected the Banqueting Hall until within recent years the monumental manner has been demonstrated continuously. We have observed the progress through many changes, from the period when it displaced the last flicker of mediævalism, through the courtly age of the eighteenth century and the commercial epoch of the nineteenth, until the chaotic uncertainties of the present age stand out in ill-defined contrast with the principles of Hellenism. The Classic ideal demands of the artist a thorough knowledge of all that is known concerning the laws of composition ; this must form his main equipment for the creation of buildings and designs. Although the task of obtaining such knowledge is one of great magnitude, its benefits are commensurate, and such laborious studies will at least ensure scholarly architecture. We cannot to-day live the life of the Greeks, the simple terms of antique conditions can no longer apply, but the unquenchable flame of Hellenic culture shines from afar, like a guiding beacon, to cheer and uplift existence.

BRONZE SPHINX FROM CLEOPATRA'S NEEDLE, THAMES EMBANKMENT
LONDON

BIBLIOGRAPHY

ACKERMANN, R. "REPOSITORY OF ART." 1809–29.

ACKERMANN, R. "MICROCOSM OF LONDON." 1808–11.

ACKERMANN, R. "SELECTION OF ORNAMENTS." 1819.

ADAM, R. "PALACE OF DIOCLETIAN AT SPALATRO." 1764.

ADAM, R. AND J. "WORKS IN ARCHITECTURE" (3 VOLS.). 1773–1822.

ADAM, R. AND J. DRAWINGS AND DESIGNS AT THE SOANE MUSEUM.

ADAM, W. "VITRUVIUS SCOTICUS." 1720–40.

ALDRICH, H. "ELEMENTA ARCHITECTURÆ CIVILIS." 1789.

ARCHITECTURAL REVIEW (THE). VARIOUS ARTICLES AND ESSAYS.

ARCHITECTURAL PUBLICATION SOCIETY'S "DICTIONARY OF ARCHITECTURE." 1848–92.

BARRY, A. "LIFE AND WORKS OF SIR CHARLES BARRY." 1867.

BARRY, SIR CHARLES. "DESIGN FOR HOUSES OF PARLIAMENT." 1836.

BARRY, SIR CHARLES. "TRAVELLERS' CLUB HOUSE," BY W. H. LEEDS. 1839.

BARRY, SIR CHARLES. "ARCHITECTURAL CAREER OF," BY M. D. WYATT. MS. 1860.

BARRY, E. M. "LECTURES ON ARCHITECTURE." 1881.

BELCHER AND MACARTNEY. "LATER RENAISSANCE ARCHITECTURE IN ENGLAND." 1898–99.

BIRCH, G. H. "LONDON CHURCHES OF THE SEVENTEENTH AND EIGHTEENTH CENTURIES." 1896.

BLOMFIELD, PROF. R. T. "HISTORY OF THE RENAISSANCE IN ENGLAND." 1900.

BONOMI, J. (THE ELDER), "MEMOIR," BY W. PAPWORTH. MS. 1869.

BRETTINGHAM (M.) "PLANS OF HOLKHAM IN NORFOLK." 1761.

BRITTON AND PUGIN. "ILLUSTRATIONS OF THE PUBLIC BUILDINGS OF LONDON AND SUPPLEMENT," BY W. H. LEEDS. 1825–38.

BUILDER, THE. 1843 *ad passim*.

CAMPBELL, COLIN. "VITRUVIUS BRITANNICUS" WITH CONTINUATION BY R. WOOLFE AND J. GANDON (5 VOLS.). 1717–25.

CAMBRIDGE. DRAWINGS IN UNIVERSITY LIBRARY AND FITZWILLIAM MUSEUM.

CASTELL, R. "VILLAS OF THE ANCIENTS." 1728.

CATES, A. BIOGRAPHICAL NOTICE OF PENNETHORNE. MS. 1871.

CHAMBERS, SIR WILLIAM. "DESIGNS OF CHINESE BUILDINGS." 1757.

CHAMBERS, SIR WILLIAM. "PLANS OF THE GARDENS AND BUILDINGS AT KEW." 1763.

CHAMBERS, SIR WILLIAM. "A DISSERTATION ON ORIENTAL GARDENING." 1772.

CHAMBERS, SIR WILLIAM. "TREATISE ON THE DECORATIVE PART OF CIVIL ARCHITECTURE." 1791. DITTO WITH "NOTES AND ESSAY ON GRECIAN ARCHITECTURE," BY J. GWILT. 1825.

CHANDLER, R. "TRAVELS IN ASIA MINOR AND GREECE" (2 VOLS.). 1807.

CHATEAUNEUF (A. DE). "ARCHITECTURA DOMESTICA." 1839.

CHATEAUNEUF (A. DE). "ARCHITECTURA PUBLICA." 1860.

"CIVIL ENGINEER AND ARCHITECTS' JOURNAL" (THE). 1837–74.

CLAYTON, J. "WORKS OF SIR CHRISTOPHER WREN." 1848–49.

COCKBURN (COL.) AND DONALDSON, T. L. "POMPEII ILLUSTRATED." 1827.

COCKERELL, PROF. C. R. LECTURES AT THE ROYAL ACADEMY.

COCKERELL, PROF. C. R. COLLECTION OF DRAWINGS AT SOUTH KENSINGTON MUSEUM.

COLLARD, W. "VIEWS IN NEWCASTLE-ON-TYNE." 1842.

CRACE (THE), COLLECTION OF LONDON PRINTS AND DRAWINGS AT THE BRITISH MUSEUM, LONDON.

CRESY, MRS. E. "LIVES OF CELEBRATED ARCHITECTS," TRANSLATED FROM F. MILIZIA. 1826.

CRUNDEN, J. "CONVENIENT AND ORNAMENTAL ARCHITECTURE." 1770.

CUNNINGHAM, ALAN. "LIVES OF THE MOST EMINENT BRITISH PAINTERS, SCULPTORS AND ARCHITECTS" (6 VOLS.). 1829–33.

CUST, LIONEL AND COLVIN, SIDNEY. "HISTORY OF THE SOCIETY OF DILETTANTI." 1898.

DANCE, G. "LIFE OF," BY S. ANGELL. 1847.

DICTIONARY OF ARCHITECTURE. "ARCHITECTURAL PUBLICATION SOCIETY." 1848–92.

DOBSON, M. J. "MEMOIR OF JOHN DOBSON." 1885.

DONALDSON, PROF. T. L. COLLECTION OF DRAWINGS AT UNIVERSITY COLLEGE, LONDON.

DONALDSON, PROF. T. L. LECTURES AND VARIOUS PAPERS DEALING WITH THE LIVES OF ARCHITECTS.

DUBLIN. "VIEWS OF BUILDINGS," BY POOL AND CASH. 1780.

DURAND, J. W. L. "RECUEIL ET PARALLÈLE DES ÉDIFICES." 1801–9.

DURAND, J. W. L. "LECONS D'ARCHITECTURE." 1821–23.

BIBLIOGRAPHY

EDINBURGH IN THE NINETEENTH CENTURY. T. H. SHEPHERD. 1829.

ELMES, J. LECTURES ON ARCHITECTURE. 1821.

ELMES, J. "LIFE AND WORKS OF SIR CHRISTOPHER WREN." 1823.

ELMES, J. "DICTIONARY OF THE FINE ARTS." 1826.

ELMES, J. "TOPOGRAPHICAL DICTIONARY OF LONDON." 1831.

ELMES, J. AND SHEPHERD. "METROPOLITAN IMPROVEMENTS." 1827.

EVELYN, J. "DIARY OF JOHN EVELYN."

EVELYN, J. "PARALLEL OF ANCIENT AND MODERN ARCHITECTURE," TRANSLATED FROM FREART. 1680.

FERGUSSON, J. "THE BRITISH MUSEUM, NATIONAL GALLERY AND NATIONAL RECORD OFFICE, WITH SUGGESTIONS FOR THEIR IMPROVEMENT." 1849.

FERGUSSON, J. "HISTORY OF ARCHITECTURE IN ALL COUNTRIES" (5 VOLS.).

FITZWILLIAM MUSEUM, CAMBRIDGE. DRAWINGS AND LETTERS OF PROF. COCKERELL AND BASEVI.

FLAXMAN, J. LECTURES ON SCULPTURE DELIVERED BEFORE THE ROYAL ACADEMY.

FOULSTON, J. "PUBLIC BUILDINGS IN THE WEST OF ENGLAND." 1838.

FREART, R. "PARALLEL OF THE ANCIENT ARCHITECTURE WITH THE MODERN," TRANSLATED BY JOHN EVELYN. 1680.

GANDON, J. "LIFE OF," BY T. J. MULVANY. 1846.

GANDY, J. P. "POMPEII," BY SIR WILLIAM GELL AND J. P. GANDY. 1827.

GENTLEMAN'S MAGAZINE 1780 ad passim.

GELL, SIR WILLIAM. See GANDY.

GIBBS, J. "BOOK OF ARCHITECTURE." 1728.

GIBBS, J. "RULES FOR DRAWING THE FIVE ORDERS." 1732.

GIBBS, J. "BIBLIOTHECA RADCLIVIANA." 1747.

GOLDICUTT, J. "SPECIMENS OF ANCIENT DECORATIONS FROM POMPEII." 1825.

GOLDICUTT, J. VOLUME OF DESIGNS IN THE LIBRARY OF THE ROYAL INSTITUTE OF BRITISH ARCHITECTS.

GREEK REVIVAL (THE). MANUSCRIPT BY J. WOOD IN THE LIBRARY OF THE ARCHITECTURAL ASSOCIATION.

HOPE, THOMAS. "HOUSEHOLD FURNITURE AND INTERIOR DECORATION." 1807.

HOPE, THOMAS. "HISTORICAL ESSAY ON ARCHITECTURE." 1835.

"ILLUSTRATED LONDON NEWS." 1850 ad passim

INIGO JONES'S DESIGNS, (2 VOLS. FOLIO). 1727.

INWOOD, H. W. "THE ERECHTHEION AT ATHENS." 1827.

LAING, D. "PLANS, ETC., OF BUILDINGS, PUBLIC AND PRIVATE, INCLUDING THE NEW CUSTOM HOUSE, LONDON." 1818.

LE ROY. "LES RUINES DES PLUS BEAUX MONUMENTS DE LA GRÈCE." 1758.

LEWIS, J. "DESIGNS IN ARCHITECTURE." 1780-97.

LOUDON, J. C. "THE ARCHITECTURAL MAGAZINE." 1838.

"LONDINA ILLUSTRATA." R. WILKINSON. 1819-25.

"LONDON IN THE NINETEENTH CENTURY," BY T. H. SHEPHERD AND J. ELMES. 1827-29.

"LONDON, PAST AND PRESENT." WHEATLEY AND CUNNINGHAM.

"LONDON INTERIORS." 1841.

"LONDON AND ITS VICINITY." T. WEALE. 1851.

MALTON, JAMES. "PICTURESQUE TOUR THROUGH THE CITIES OF LONDON AND WESTMINSTER." 1792.

"METROPOLITAN IMPROVEMENTS; OR, LONDON IN THE NINETEENTH CENTURY." SHEPHERD AND ELMES. 1828.

MICHAELIS, A. "ANCIENT MARBLES IN GREAT BRITAIN." 1882.

NEALE, J. P. "VIEWS OF SEATS OF NOBLEMEN AND GENTLEMEN OF GREAT BRITAIN AND IRELAND." 1824-29.

NEEDHAM, R. AND WEBSTER, J. "SOMERSET HOUSE, PAST AND PRESENT." 1905.

PAINE, J. "PLANS, ETC., OF THE MANSION HOUSE, DONCASTER." 1751.

PAINE, J. "PLANS OF NOBLEMEN'S AND GENTLEMEN'S HOUSES, ETC." 1767-83.

PALLADIO. "FIRST BOOK OF ARCHITECTURE," TRANSLATED BY G. RICHARDS. 1693.

PAPWORTH, WYATT. PECULIAR CHARACTERISTICS OF THE PALLADIAN SCHOOL OF ARCHITECTURE. MS. 1848.

"PARENTALIA OF SIR CHRISTOPHER WREN." BY STEPHEN WREN. 1750.

PEPYS, SAMUEL. "DIARY."

PIRANESI. VARIOUS ETCHINGS AND DESIGNS. 1748-78.

"PIRANESI." BY ARTHUR SAMUEL. 1910.

PYNE, W. H. "HISTORY OF THE ROYAL RESIDENCES." 1819.

REDGRAVE, J. "DICTIONARY OF ARTISTS OF THE ENGLISH SCHOOL." 1878.

RENNIE, SIR J. "AUTOBIOGRAPHY." 1875.

REYNOLDS, SIR JOSHUA. "DISCOURSES GIVEN AT THE ROYAL ACADEMY."

RICHARDSON, G. "BOOK OF CEILINGS, ENGLISH AND FRENCH TEXT." 1776.

RICHARDSON, G. "NEW COLLECTION OF CHIMNEY-PIECES." 1781.

BIBLIOGRAPHY

RICHARDSON, G. "FIVE ORDERS OF ARCHITECTURE." 1787.

RICHARDSON, G. "NEW DESIGNS IN ARCHITECTURE." 1792.

RICHARDSON, G. "NEW VITRUVIUS BRITANNICUS" (2 VOLS.). 1802-8.

ROYAL INSTITUTE OF BRITISH ARCHITECTS, THE. "TRANSACTIONS," 1837 *ad passim*.

ROYAL INSTITUTE OF BRITISH ARCHITECTS, THE. COLLECTIONS OF DRAWINGS AND MANUSCRIPTS.

SANDBY, T. SIX LECTURES ON ARCHITECTURE READ AT THE ROYAL ACADEMY. 1768.

SANDBY, W. "THOMAS AND PAUL SANDBY, ROYAL ACADEMICIANS, SOME ACCOUNT OF THEIR LIVES AND WORKS." 1892.

SCHINKEL, C. VON. "SAMMLUNG ARCHITECTONISCHER ENTWÜRFE." 1819-48.

SHEPHERD, T. H. "EDINBURGH IN THE NINETEENTH CENTURY." 1829.

SHEPHERD, T. H. AND ELMES. *See* "METROPOLITAN IMPROVEMENTS."

SHUTE, JOHN. "FIRST AND CHIEF GROUNDES OF ARCHITECTURE." 1563.

SOANE, SIR JOHN. "DESIGNS IN ARCHITECTURE." 1778.

SOANE, SIR JOHN. "PLANS OF BUILDINGS EXECUTED IN THE COUNTIES OF NORFOLK, SUFFOLK, ETC. ETC." 1788.

SOANE, SIR JOHN. "DESIGNS FOR PUBLIC AND PRIVATE BUILDINGS." 1822.

SOANE, SIR JOHN, LIFE OF, BY J. BRITTON. 1834.

SOANE, SIR JOHN. LECTURES AT THE ROYAL ACADEMY.

SOANE MUSEUM. THE DRAWINGS, MANUSCRIPTS, AND PAPERS THERE.

"SOCIETY OF DILETTANTI, HISTORY OF," BY LIONEL CUST AND SYDNEY COLVIN. 1898.

SOCIETY OF DILETTANTI. VARIOUS PUBLICATIONS CONCERNING GREEK ARCHITECTURE.

STUART AND REVETT. "ANTIQUITIES OF ATHENS" (2 VOLS.). 1762, 1787. VOL. III. EDITED BY J. REVELEY. 1794. VOL. IV. EDITED BY J. WOODS. 1816. SUPPLEMENT BY C. R. COCKERELL, T. L. DONALDSON, W. JENKINS, W. KINNAIRD, AND W. RAILTON. 1830.

STRATTON, ARTHUR. "THE LIFE WORK AND INFLUENCE OF SIR CHRISTOPHER WREN." 1897.

TALLIS, F. "EXAMPLES OF LONDON AND PROVINCIAL STREET ARCHITECTURE." 1861.

TATHAM, C. H. "ETCHINGS REPRESENTING THE BEST EXAMPLES OF ANCIENT ORNAMENTAL ARCHITECTURE." 1794-96.

TAYLOR, G. L., AND CRESY, E. "ARCHITECTURAL ANTIQUITIES OF ROME" (2 VOLS.). 1821-22.

TAYLOR, A. T. "THE TOWERS AND SPIRES DESIGNED BY SIR CHRISTOPHER WREN." 1881.

TELFORD, W. "LIFE OF," EDITED BY J. RICKMAN. 1858.

VANBRUGH, SIR JOHN. "LIFE AND WORKS OF," BY E. H. BROWNE. MS. 1834.

VICTORIA AND ALBERT MUSEUM. COLLECTION OF PRINTS AND DRAWINGS.

VULLIAMY, L. "EXAMPLES OF ORNAMENTAL SCULPTURE IN ARCHITECTURE." 1825.

WALPOLE, HORACE, "ANECDOTES" AND "LETTERS."

WARE, ISAAC. "COMPLETE BODY OF ARCHITECTURE." 1756.

WEALE, J. "ORNAMENTAL IRONWORK IN THE ROYAL PARKS, ETC." 1840.

WEALE, J. "LONDON AND ITS VICINITY." 1851.

WHEATLEY AND CUNNINGHAM. "LONDON PAST AND PRESENT."

WHEATLEY, H. B. "ROUND ABOUT PICCADILLY AND PALL MALL." 1870.

WIGHTWICK, G. "AUTOBIOGRAPHY OF G. WIGHTWICK, MISCELLANEOUS PAPERS, ESSAYS AND LECTURES."

WILKINS, W. "THE ANTIQUITIES OF MAGNA GRÆCIA." 1807.

WINCKELMANN, J. "REMARQUES SUR L'ARCHITECTURE DES ANCIENS" (2 VOLS.). 1766.

WOOD, R. "RUINS OF PALMYRA." 1753.

WOOD, R. "RUINS OF BAALBEC." 1757.

WYATT, B. "DESIGN FOR THE THEATRE ROYAL, DRURY LANE, 1812." 1812.

WYATVILLE, SIR J. "LIFE OF," BY J. BRITTON. 1839.

INDEX

INDEX

INDEX

INDEX

INDEX

INDEX

INDEX

INDEX

INDEX